PRAISE FOR *LACKS SELF-CONTROL*

"Frank, fearless, and very funny."
—Arianna Huffington

"*Lacks Self-Control* is hysterical, relatable, full of truth, and unexpectedly poignant. Roy Sekoff is a seriously funny writer; his book is brimming with hilarious lines and witty wordplay. I especially enjoyed the way he captures the confusing cocktail of excitement and anxiety so often shaken and stirred by adolescent sexual awakening. It's like a modern *Portnoy's Complaint*, only WAY funnier. I loved these stories; I think you will, too."
—Jay Roach

"Roy Sekoff is living proof that ADHD, OCD, and TMI can be of great value to the betterment of mankind."
—Rob Reiner

"I've known Roy for years as a professional, put-together, successful new-media pioneer. After reading his book, I'm so happy to find out I was wrong. He's every bit as deranged as the rest of us. Plus he's really funny."
—Adam McKay

"I've read worse."
—Larry David

LACKS SELF-CONTROL

*True Stories I Waited Until
My Parents Died to Tell*

ROY SEKOFF

BIG A
BOOKS

Published by Big A Books, Los Angeles, California
www.roysekoff.com

 Edited and Designed by Girl Friday Productions
www.girlfridayproductions.com

Editorial: Emilie Sandoz-Voyer, Rebecca Jaynes, and Patty Ann Economos
Interior Design: Rachel Marek
Cover Design: Alban Fischer
Image Credits: cover © STUDIOGRANDOUEST/iStock;
© Denys Kurbatov/Adobe Stock

ISBN (Hardcover): 978-0-9998927-0-1
ISBN (Paperback): 978-0-9998927-1-8
e-ISBN: 978-0-9998927-2-5

First Edition

Printed in the United States of America

For my parents
who supported me
long after it made sense to do so

Contents

The Story of These Stories

After seventeen years of dancing to the rhythms of the 24/7 news cycle, eleven of them as the founding editor of the Huffington Post, I decided to try a different beat.

Thankfully, the success of HuffPost afforded me the rare luxury to allow my mind—and my body—to wander.

As my always-revved inner motor slowly downshifted, I relearned what it was like to not place "respond to 50 emails" at the top of my daily to-do list—ahead of "brush teeth" and "empty bladder"—and to revel in the sublime satisfaction of snagging a prime spot in the carpool line at my daughter's school.

I knew that before I could figure out who I was outside of my role at HuffPost, I needed the mental equivalent of the Master Cleanse—heavy on the cayenne pepper.

So, for months, I willfully resisted all creative urges, stubbing out even the spark of any idea that might grow into a concept or, perish the thought, an actual endeavor.

Eventually, my psychological detox accomplished, I began to contemplate what I might want to do next. And what I realized was: I had no freaking clue what I should do next! Free to con-sider anything, I came up with nothing.

Then, without warning, my unconscious decided to get involved. But it didn't tap me on the shoulder and whisper *Hi, Roy, have you thought about . . . ?* No, it came rushing up to me like a crazy person on the street, shrieking in my ear: *HEY, ASSHOLE . . . DO THIS!!!*

Every day for a week, I woke up in the middle of the night—often multiple times—my mind racing with ideas. It wasn't a manic episode—but you could definitely see manic from where I was standing (or, more accurately, sitting up in bed). Not want-ing to forget these late-night musings, I started sending myself emails with notes about stories I wanted to tell. Stories from my life. Some of these were tried-and-true tales I'd been telling over dinner or drinks for years. Some were stories I'd only told my closest confidants. And some were stories I hadn't even thought about for decades.

Night after night, story idea after story idea. One night, I sent myself thirteen different emails between 2:00 and 5:30 a.m. I soon realized that if I ever hoped to get a decent night's sleep again, I was going to have to get these stories out of my head and onto paper.

This book is the result.

Since many of the stories are about things that happened in the early years of my life, as part of the writing process, I dug through a collection of papers and mementos my mother had squirreled away, hoping to fact-check a few memories and kick loose some others.

A trove of well-preserved report cards proved particularly enlightening.

It seems that my essential character was in place quite early. According to my preschool teacher, four-year-old me had "a wonderful sense of humor which is enjoyed by all—including his teacher!" (Although I apparently had "trouble coloring inside the lines" and was only "fair" with scissors.) And my first-grade teacher noted: "Roy enjoys creative writing and should be encouraged to do so more often."

So, by the age of seven, I was showing signs of being a funny writer. Why the hell did I then spend so much of the ensuing three decades in existential turmoil, struggling to figure out what I should be doing with my life?

The one thing all my teachers seem to have agreed on was that I desperately needed to *sit still and shut the fuck up.*

Year after year, grading period after grading period, I continually got check marks for Lacks Self-Control ("A check mark indicates the pupil needs improvement"). In the "Additional Comments" section, my teachers sounded like a broken record:

> Kindergarten: "Although he's generally agreeable, Roy lacks self-control."
> First grade: "Roy is often too talkative and disturbs others."
> Second grade: "Roy needs to work on his self-control."
> Third grade: "Moving forward, Roy should try to reduce his talking and excessive movements."
> Fourth grade: "It would be most helpful if Roy would practice more self-control."
> Fifth grade: "Roy often talks too much, thus sacrificing quality of work."

Sixth grade: "Roy verbalizes about improving his behavior but for the most part does little about it."

At the time, I wore those check marks like a scarlet letter. But from the vantage point of middle age, it feels more like a badge of honor.

Indeed, as I mentally fast-forward through the movie of my life, I see that, without planning to, I have made Lacks Self-Control something of a guiding philosophy.

That's not to imply that I habitually act impulsively, or recklessly say and do things without considering the consequences. For me, Lacks Self-Control means:

- Speaking up and speaking out. Not only saying that the emperor has no clothes, but also pointing out that his penis is smaller than average.
- Refusing to stay in your assigned seat when there's a parade passing by outside the window.
- Being willing to risk looking foolish—and embracing it when you do.
- Not self-censoring (there's already an ample supply of folks eager to do it for you).
- Taking the road less traveled—even though it often has massive potholes, scary-looking hitchhikers, and many long, lonely stretches.
- Frequently asking *Why?*
- Frequently saying *Why not!*
- Questioning authority—whether it's your tightly wound eighth-grade history teacher or a tight-fisted executive

who'd rather say yes to a proven mediocrity than an innovative but unproven new idea.

- Understanding that daydreaming isn't wasting time; it's a high-intensity workout for your imagination.
- And never, *ever* passing up a killer punch line—whether it pops into your head at a parent-teacher conference for your kid or while pitching a $30 million project to a stone-faced board of directors.

In baseball, they say that a tie goes to the runner. In my brain, when competing impulses are racing to the bag—my superego saying *maybe you shouldn't,* my id saying *go on, give it a shot*—the tie goes to the id.

I guess I'm still having trouble coloring inside the lines.

This approach to life has landed me in a fair share of sticky situations over the years (see many of the escapades herein), and produced a lifetime of shaken heads, tsk-tsks, and "I can't believe you just did/said that" reactions.

But it has also led to a lot of laughs, very few boring days, and a bunch of stories I think are worth sharing.*

Maybe now I can finally get some sleep.

These stories are all true—at least as true as the tricks of memory will allow. In an effort to avoi• unpleasant future legal entanglements, some names and identifying details have been changed.

Dirty Projectors

When my puberty starter kit arrived in February 1972, I didn't know whether to sign for it, mark it "Return to Sender," or tear open the box like a much-anticipated birthday gift (*Pubic hair? Just what I wanted!*).

All things considered, I was shockingly naive about what was happening to my body.

I had a father, an older brother, a variety of grown-up male cousins, a couple of precocious friends, and had sat through those school "health ed" lectures where the girls went to one room to hear about training bras and menstruation while the boys were told about deeper voices, pimples, and "nocturnal emissions." But even with all that, no one had ever cut to the chase and explained the rudimentary jerk-off equation: get turned on, grasp erect penis, stroke, ejaculate, dispose of tissue. Repeat as needed.

Of course, step one—"get turned on"—wasn't an issue in those early days. Indeed, the real challenge was getting turned *off* enough to make it through the day without sporting wood in carpool, on the PE field, or during my twice-weekly bar mitzvah prep lessons (*sorry, Rabbi, but for some reason reading the haftorah makes me think of Peggy Lipton*).

Even so, I soon realized that adding porn and/or sexual fantasies to the masturbatory mix was key in taking my self-pleasure game to the next level.

Luckily for me, my father turned out to be something of an erotica aficionado. A devotee of the dirty. And while he didn't flaunt his penchant for the prurient, he didn't go out of his way to hide it either.

When I was younger, I'd sometimes spot a copy of *Playboy* tucked discreetly into his desk drawer. By the time I hit puberty, they were more conspicuous; he kept a small pile of back issues on a bottom shelf in his book-lined study. The room's layout was like a psychograph of his varied passions: the high shelves contained some of the great works of literature, history, philosophy, and psychology; in the middle were detective novels, biographies, and books on the movies; and, down below, the girlie mags.

These magazines became my gateway drug to the broader world of "adult entertainment." It started with *Playboy*, but the more risqué *Penthouse* was soon added to the low-shelf collection. If *Playboy* was the Beatles of men's magazines—cute, cheeky, fresh-faced—*Penthouse* was the Rolling Stones: darker, edgier, lewder.

The early '70s was the heyday of high-gloss photographic filth—and it seemed like every few months brought a new occupant to the bottom shelf, with *Playboy* and *Penthouse* eventually joined by *Oui, Club, Cheri, High Society, Swank, Chic, Gallery*, and, pushing as many cultural buttons as it could, *Hustler*.

These all fueled my fantasies—and my barely controllable desire to, as the great wits of seventh grade liked to call it, "make a date with Rosie Palm and her five sisters."

But something told me there were even nastier thrills to be found. So, like a horny archeologist, I set out to excavate what I hoped would be the smut equivalent of King Tut's tomb: my father's closet.

The next time my parents went out to dinner, I slunk into my dad's half of the large hallway closet he and my mother shared. And, like one of the bloodhounds sniffing out escaped cons Tony Curtis and Sidney Poitier in *The Defiant Ones*, I quickly homed in on what I was looking for: a stash of Super 8 stag films.

My heart pounding, I suddenly hesitated, wondering: Was I about to open a door best left shut? Was this more than my twelve-year-old brain could handle? And what about the invasion of my father's privacy; was this akin to reading someone's diary?

The anticipation boner pressing against my leg was all the answer I needed. Damn, it's my torpedo: full speed ahead!

On a high shelf, I spotted the projector my dad had occasionally carted out to screen home movies. It was an old-school Bell & Howell model that was advertised as "portable" but, as I soon found out, weighed approximately the same as a forging anvil. I could barely get it down from the shelf, and banged it against my head in the process.

But that was just the start of the difficulties I encountered. Once I managed to remove the protective case (elapsed time: five minutes), I came face-to-face with a mechanism only slightly less complicated than the Apollo Lunar Module. The owner's manual was equally daunting, with page after page of instructions on "maintaining an adequate film loop" and making sure "the ratchet sprockets are fully engaged." Jesus, I just wanted to watch people fuck, not learn a new trade!

Making matters worse, I kept hearing what I thought was the sound of car doors slamming—the signal that my parents were home. So I'd scurry to the window, see that it wasn't them, and scurry back. I didn't get this good a workout in Coach Miller's third-period PE class, and he was a sadistic bastard who made us run extra laps around the playing field if anyone forgot their gym clothes—which someone always did.

I reluctantly decided to abort my lecherous mission and regroup. With great effort, I returned the projector to its high shelf, once more bumping my head as I did. And I put back the two Super 8 reels I'd planned to watch, leaving them *exactly* as I'd found them (over time I developed an attention to detail that would rival the world's most meticulous spies). But I took the projector's instruction manual with me, vowing that I was going to understand that sucker better than either Bell *or* Howell.

And, after many hours of intensive study—the phrase "a man possessed" was first used to describe my work mastering the Bell & Howell—I did just that, gaining entry into a flickering, silent, Triple-X world in which dentists filled cavities and drilled vaginas; plumbers unclogged sinks, then got their snakes drained; and bored college roommates would decide to pass the time sharing a double-ended dildo. It was a land populated with suspiciously mature-looking European schoolgirls, masturbating housewives, horny babysitters, naughty nurses, and pizza delivery guys getting a very special tip.

I used every mental defense mechanism at my disposal to completely separate the dirty movies I was watching from the fact that they belonged to my dad. But, given a deeply disturbing incident four years earlier, I was pleased to detect no discernible pattern or favored fetish in his collection.

The trauma had occurred when I was eight, during a sleepover at my best friend Stu's house, after we discovered Stu's older brother Terry and his pal Roger surreptitiously watching what we assumed were home movies. When they refused to let us join them, Stu unleashed one of the strongest weapons in the sibling arsenal: "If you don't let us see what you're watching, I'll tell Mom and Dad!"

Terry responded with one of his big guns: "If you don't leave us alone, I'll beat the crap out of you!"

Terry and Stu eyed each other closely, each weighing the potential downside of their share of this brotherly take on Mutually Assured Destruction. The impasse was broken by Roger, who said, "Why don't we just show them. Who gives a rat's ass?"

Terry and Roger huddled by the projector, talking it over. Finally, Terry turned to us and said, "Suit yourself" and restarted the film.

I turned my head to the screen, expecting to see Stu's parents bringing him home from the hospital, or Terry playing second base in a Little League game, or footage from the trip our families took together to Nassau.

I didn't expect to see a plump, fair-haired woman I didn't recognize sitting on a couch getting her private parts licked by a dog. I stared at the screen, utterly dumbfounded. It was like you'd handed me a book to read, but it was in Chinese. Or Martian. This did not compute. There were so many dissonant images to process. I'd never actually seen a naked woman before, and certainly not one holding her vagina open while a mutt of indeterminate breed lapped at it like it was a bowl of water and he'd just come in from a long, hot run.

Things got even more confusing when the woman got on her hands and knees while Fido tried to mount her from behind. It apparently wasn't going well, so a skeevy-looking man stepped into the frame to help the dog out. That must've worked because the canine began furiously humping away. The woman seemed distracted—bored, even.

I was anything but bored. But I wasn't getting turned on either. It's not like I wasn't curious about sex or the differences between boys and girls. I remember, as a five-year-old, furtively stripping the clothes off a neighbor girl's Barbie, hoping to get a clue what a naked woman looked like, and being sadly disappointed upon seeing the doll's detail-free crotch.

My ignorance was largely circumstantial. I had been cast adrift in a sea of XY chromosomes. I had no sisters, no female cousins, and there were only two girls in the whole neighborhood—and both of them were older than me. One of them was Shelley, the pretty daughter of my dad's best friend. She was fourteen, had long brown hair that hung to her waist, and had been the object of my first vaguely erotic thoughts.

One time, I was over at her house and she invited me into her room to play Mystery Date, the board game in which the players, theoretically young girls, try to win a date with a "dreamboat" and not a "dud." At some point, her mother came in and told her she needed to change into a dress for a party they were going to. Shelley nodded in my direction and said, "I can't until he goes." To which her mother replied, "Don't be silly, it's only Roy." I held my breath, secretly crossed my fingers and toes, and, feeling a tingling in my prepubescent loins, prepared for the unveiling. But Shelley insisted on my removal, and I was escorted out the door—thwarted but strangely titillated.

However, now that I found myself presented with a cinematic exploration of an actual vagina in action, albeit partnered with a doggie dick, stimulation was the furthest thing from my mind—or my groin. In fact, I wasn't focused on the naked woman at all. I just kept thinking about the dog. Is this what all dogs did when they weren't playing fetch, chasing the milkman, or begging to be petted?

My thoughts turned to our pet mutt Frisky. Was he like the pooch in the movie? I'd never thought of him that way; he wasn't even one of those dogs that would stick their nose in your crotch and sniff. I'd seen him occasionally lick his own balls, but I thought that he was just cleaning himself or trying to scratch an itch. Was he, in fact, an interspecies sex machine?

My mind then drifted to Stu's dogs, King and Kong—a pair of aggressive Norwegian Elkhounds that would never stop barking whenever I was over at his house. My first thought was the same as always: *What kind of people keep Norwegian Elkhounds in Miami, for godsakes?* But my second thought was new and disturbing: Were King and Kong also labia lappers and people fuckers? I couldn't stop from mentally replacing the woman in the movie with Stu's mother, a thickset bottle blonde who owned a gift shop. Would she, when she was feeling lonely, light one of the heart-shaped scented candles she sold and bring King and Kong into her bedroom?

My mind thankfully refused to perform the same recasting exercise using my mother. But I was finding it hard to not consider the possibility that I was living in a world far more depraved than I'd ever imagined.

My twisted reverie was cut short when the last of the porn film ran through the gate and out the back of the projector. Terry clicked off the bulb, while Roger turned on the room lights.

"Welcome to the wonderful world of dirty movies," he said with a laugh. "But don't say anything to your mom and dad, or we'll all be up Shit Creek without a paddle!"

Stu and I both nodded. But Roger needn't have worried. I would sooner have been tortured by the Nazi spies or *Creature Feature* mutants who sometimes haunted my childhood nightmares than talk about what I'd just seen with anyone—let alone my parents.

Later, as I lay in the top bunk of Stu's double-decker bed, I found myself pondering where the doggie-porn flick had come from. Did it belong to Stu's father, a balding stockbroker who looked like he always needed a shave? And, if so, was it something he only busted out for his buddies' stag parties, or did he get a kinky kick out of watching a dog lick the crotch of a bored, frumpy stranger? This was way more than my eight-year-old brain could handle, but, as I drifted off to sleep, I could already feel the psychic scar starting to form.

That's why twelve-year-old me was so relieved to uncover no canine leading men among my dad's collection of raunch. I found it comforting to know that he was a perv but not a deviant.

Despite my hard-earned expertise, the Bell & Howell projector was still a finicky, often maddening contraption. Besides being heavy and hard to thread, it required repeated refocusing and was always in danger of having the film come off the sprockets. And it was noisier than a person in my position would prefer. Besides possibly calling attention to my secretive forays into Smutville, the sound of the film moving through the machine made it hard to hear if my parents were coming home. So, during these filthy film-fests, my central nervous system was usually redlining—a jittery combination of turned on and terrified. It should come as no surprise that for many years I associated titillation with dread, not exactly the foundation for a healthy approach to intimacy.

Because of these issues, I reserved my use of the projector to special occasions when I knew my parents would be out for a significant stretch. Dinner wasn't enough. Dinner and a movie, and it was showtime. They rarely went out of town; but if they did, it invariably led to a movie—and subsequent masturbation—marathon.

One night, when I knew my parents would be out late, I made my way downstairs to see if there were any new arrivals in the closet. I'm not sure how it worked—whether my dad got the 8mm loops via mail order or at a local adult bookstore—but there was a fairly frequent turnover of the collection. This engendered a complicated mix of emotions: the thrill of a new discovery, tinged with sadness over the departure of a longtime favorite (good-bye mischievous maid with the magical vacuum cleaner attachment!).

Pushing aside the hanging shirts that concealed the closet's mini red-light district, I instantly spotted a new, unmarked reel (sometimes they would come in labeled boxes—"The Dr. Is In!"— sometimes it was more of a crapshoot). I never liked these mystery flicks, always worried that I might see something that could permanently scar my impressionable psyche. But I'd seen all the other selections—multiple times—and decided to roll the dice.

I needn't have worried. It was a pretty standard-issue girl-on-girl flick, with very little "plot." One girl catches the other one playing with herself and decides to join in. Kissing, grinding, fingering, and licking ensue. The usual. What wasn't usual was what happened halfway in, just as the gals were moving into a little run of 69: a section of the film got caught in the gate, and the image on the screen—lips approaching pubic hair—froze. Pouncing like a jungle cat, I tried to flip the projector into "Reverse," but only succeeded in trapping the film more firmly in the gate. I watched in horror as Girl #1's bush blistered, bubbled, then melted away. The screen went white as the film snapped in two, the take-up reel spinning rapidly.

Oh. Dear. God. No!!!

The doomsday scenario—a badly damaged film, butchered on my watch—had come to pass. With rising panic, I scrambled to consider my options:

1. I could try to repair the film, cutting out the damaged frames and splicing the rest together (snag: I didn't have the required splicing equipment or know-how to do this).
2. I could skip the splicing, hand-rewind the film so the two halves overlapped, and hope that when my dad played it he'd think the break was his fault (snag: the melted and mangled footage was more incriminating than the missing frames from the Zapruder film).
3. Why couldn't I think of any better options?!

Then it hit me: what if I simply made the lesbian loop vanish? Would my father even realize it was missing—and if so, what would he think happened to it? Would he immediately pinpoint me as the prime suspect or would he question himself, wondering if he'd already returned it and just didn't remember?

This seemed like the best worst option, so I sprang into action, briskly putting Operation Gaslight Dad into effect. First, I procured a large garbage bag. Then, I unspooled the half of the film still on the Bell & Howell's return reel into the bag (it was a tangled mess and took up a lot more room than expected) and shoved the other half into the bag.

After hurrying to put the projector back in its place, I took the bag and slipped out the side door. Since it was getting late, and I was still four years away from being able to drive, I decided the best place to dump the evidence was in the bay behind our house. Having seen my share of gangster movies, I knew I needed to weigh down the "body" before sending it to its watery grave.

So I loaded the bag with rocks and, saying a little prayer that the bag didn't rip, took a run-up worthy of an Olympic javelin champ and heaved it into the water.

For a tantalizing and terrible moment, the bag floated on the surface; shit, maybe celluloid was more buoyant than I'd anticipated! But, eventually, the rocks and gravity did their job and the bag dipped under the water, sinking to the bottom of the bay. The masturbating gal and her sapphic sweetie now swam with the fishes (who hopefully would appreciate some hot Super 8 girl-on-girl action).

In the end, my father never said anything to me. Either Operation Gaslight Dad had worked, or he'd decided to give me a break. Even in later years, when our relationship had matured into more of a friendship, I never asked him if he'd known what I was up to.

You might think the traumatic nature of the incident—which I came to think of as the Melting Muff Episode—would've had a chilling effect. But it wasn't long before I was slipping back into the hallway closet, eager for another clandestine encounter with the balky Bell & Howell.

Somewhere, the porn equivalent of Darth Vader was looking down on me and thinking: "The libidinous Force is strong with this one."

scωl dæɤ

I went to an experimental elementary school. So the administration felt it was their right—indeed, their duty—to treat us like scholastic guinea pigs.

Some of these educational experiments were benign, like grouping students from multiple grades in "classroom pods" or an early trial run of televised Spanish classes featuring an impassioned instructor who would roll her *R*s like a woman possessed, beseeching us to repeat what she'd just said: *"R-r-r-r-r-r-r-r-epite, por favor!!"*

But some had far-reaching consequences, such as the decision to teach students to read using a new—and supposedly improved—alphabet. That's right, some pedagogic visionary thought it would be a good idea to teach seven-year-olds to read using an untested phonetic alphabet that featured forty-four symbols instead of the standard twenty-six letters. The idea was that this so-called Initial Teaching Alphabet (i.t.a.) would get its users reading faster—and with more confidence—at which point they would "move seamlessly" into the normal alphabet.

And the forward-thinking honchos at Henry S. West Laboratory School (aka "West Lab"), always looking to traverse the cutting edge of learning, jumped at the chance to give it a shot (of course, *they* could already read, so no skin off their nut sacks, right?).

My fellow first graders and I were chosen to be our school's test pilots.

And, initially, things went swimmingly for me. I was like a reading Chuck Yeager. Since every vowel or consonant sound had a corresponding symbol, I didn't have to figure out if the letter *A* represented the "short A sound" as in "cat" or the "long A sound" as in "cake"—or whether *ch* was meant to sound like it did in "chair" or in "ache." By the end of the school year, I was already reading at a fourth-grade level.

bravœ, i.t.a., wel dun (the new alphabet didn't use capital letters or conventional punctuation).

But like so many well-intentioned experiments before it, early success was soon dampened by unintended consequences: in my case, the fact that I became a lifelong miserable speller. After suckling at the sound-it-out teat of i.t.a., I found the vagaries of standard English never made sense to me. Why are there two *H*s in "rhythm"? Why does "harass" have one *R* but "embarrass" have two? Similarly, why does "occurred" have two *C*s and "recommend" only one? Only in a cruel and unfeeling universe would "phone" start with a *ph*. "Lieutenant"? "Architect"? "Chauffeur"? If it wasn't for spell-check, I'd never come within a diphthong of getting those words right. And who was the linguistic sadist who decided that the *k* in "knife" is silent?

Making matters worse, my subsequent teachers acted like this foray into the alphabetic unknown never happened. In fact, my second-grade teacher had the nerve to note on my progress report: "I would like to see Roy make fewer mistakes in spelling and in the use of capital letters and punctuation marks." *Really? Well, maybe you should think about that the next time you decide to treat me like an academic lab rat, inculcating my mind with a dubious alphabet that doesn't use capital letters or established punctuation.* That's like a doctor prescribing a pregnant woman thalidomide and then, at her legless infant's yearly checkup, saying he wished the kid was taller.

West Lab was a public school, but was so difficult to get into that, according to family lore, as soon as the doctor told my mother that "the rabbit died," the first thing she did, even before telling my father that she was pregnant, was drive to the registrar's office and enroll me as "Baby Sekoff (gender unknown)."

Ten years later, I had a name, male gonads, and was in the homestretch of my final year at the school.

Looking over the box of grade school report cards my mother dutifully saved, a picture of what I was like as a fledgling student starts to emerge—and it's a decidedly unremarkable portrait.

I wasn't a bad student; but anyone hoping to be valedictorian needn't bother looking over their shoulder to see if I was gaining on them. If my school had graded using words instead of letters, my GPA would've been "Meh."

And, of course, there was the unanimous, frequently expressed agreement among my teachers that I lacked self-control.

The truth is, I wasn't trying to be disruptive. I was just chafing under the one-size-fits-all approach of the American educational system, and pushing back against the autocratic authoritarianism our instructors lorded over us. Or at least that's what I told myself.

But even with crappy spelling, an indifferent attitude, and my inability to stop talking, by sixth grade I had cobbled together a solid if unspectacular elementary school resume.

I was a step below Star Student and a step above That Kid in the Class Picture You Can't Remember.

I didn't run for student council president; I was the campaign manager for the guy who won.

I didn't enter the talent show; I was recruited to be the emcee. ("You're always yattering, Sekoff," the teacher organizing the production told me. "Maybe we can finally put that to good use.")

I was never the first one picked in PE; but I was also never in the bottom half of the draft.

In short, I couldn't hold a candle to my straight-A-getting, violin-playing, no-check-marks-for-self-control older brother (indeed, I could always see the disappointment in my teachers' eyes when they realized I "wasn't another Jed"). But I *had* managed to carve out a niche for myself as a budding writer. In fact, I had recently been asked to read a poem I'd written about the need for racial harmony in front of the whole school. Titled "Together," it started: "Black and White, Yellow and Red / If we don't stick together we'll all be dead."

So I was confused and more than a little concerned when my PE teacher called me away from a highly competitive kickball game and handed me a note saying the principal, Mr. Rizzo, wanted to see me "right away."

What could this be about? I wondered as I double-timed it to his office, my face still flushed from having just legged-out a slow roller down the third-base line (we took our kickball very seriously at West Lab). Yes, I had drawn the ire of my priggish teacher, Mrs. Turner, by acting out Billy Jack's "I'm gonna take this right foot, and I'm gonna whop you on that side of your face . . . and there's not a damn thing you're gonna be able to do about it" speech during homeroom the day before, but surely that didn't rise to the level of a visit to the principal's office—especially since there was less than a week before the last day of school. Not even Mrs. Turner would be that petty . . . would she?

I knew something strange was afoot when I handed the note my PE teacher had given me to the principal's assistant—a pale-skinned older woman who had been unfailingly sweet to me over the years—and she shot me a cold, hard stare and told me to take a seat in a nearby chair.

It wasn't long before the door behind her jerked open and Mr. Rizzo, a balding, barrel-chested man in a drab, dark suit stepped out, looking down at a sheet of paper. He handed it to his assistant, told her to file it, then noticed I was there.

I slowly rose from the chair. "Coach Davis said you wanted to see me?"

He didn't respond at first; he just glared at me, a steely look in his eye. "I'll let you know when I'm ready for you," he finally said in a sandpapery rasp. "For now, I just want you to sit there and think about what you've done." He turned and went into his office, closing the door behind him.

I was baffled. What had I done? I glanced at his assistant, hoping for some clue, but she just looked away, clearly appalled.

I began racking my brain for possible infractions that might've provoked this level of ire, but all I could come up with were a series of recent misdemeanors: a giggling fit during the screening of a hippie-dippy anti-drug film; doing a half-assed job on my final science project (determining which type of music my dog hated the most); singing "Joy to the World" at full voice with three of my buddies on the way to the cafeteria ("Jeremiah was a bullfrog!!!"). And, of course, the Billy Jack Incident. Surely

23

none of those were the reason I was sitting there, trying not to shit on myself.

After an interminable wait, Mr. Rizzo reemerged and, maintaining his executioner's mien, led me into his office. He sat behind a large desk, motioning for me to take a seat in front of him.

"So what do you have to say for yourself?"

I wasn't sure if this was a trick question, but I knew I needed to be careful not to say anything that could be interpreted as "lippy," "mouthy," "smart-alecky," or even "class clowny"—all things I'd been accused of at one time or another.

"Well, sir . . . ," I said, trying not to think about how much he looked like a macho Spiro Agnew. "To be honest . . . I'm not really sure why I'm here."

He exhaled disdainfully, with so much force a small fleck of spit easily cleared his desk and would've landed on my cheek if I hadn't leaned to one side. "Please, let's not play games—you know exactly what you did . . ."

"I honestly don't."

"Of course you do."

He let this hang there, as if it was the final word on the matter. I knew I was in danger of crossing the lippy red line if I continued down the "No, I don't . . . Yes, you do" path, so I just held his gaze.

He decided to try a different tack: "So what do you think the proper punishment should be? Normally something like this would call for a suspension . . ."

"Something like what?"

He ignored me and kept going: "But so close to the end of the year, that would probably mean you wouldn't graduate."

My balls shot up into my abdomen as if they'd been launched atop a Saturn V rocket. "Are you saying I'd have to repeat sixth grade?" I said, my voice cracking.

"It's definitely a possibility. Or maybe we could settle up a different way . . ."

He glanced over at a lacquered wooden paddle with holes drilled in it, propped in the corner. West Lab had never allowed corporal punishment, but Rizzo looked like the kind of guy who thought a couple of good whacks was a perfectly fine form of schoolhouse justice.

I felt my face flush as tears began welling up in the corners of my eyes. "Look, Mr. Rizzo, I'm not trying to be smart or play games here—I truly don't know what this is about."

He shook his head in disgust, then opened his desk drawer and pulled out a small vinyl-covered autograph book, which he placed on his desk.

"You recognize this?" he asked.

"No, sir . . . Not really."

"Not really? Either you recognize it or you don't."

This was starting to sound like a bad scene from *Dragnet* (a redundancy, I know).

"I mean, I know it's an autograph book, and that some of the kids are passing them around for their friends and teachers to sign . . . I just don't know what it has to do with me."

"Oh, you don't, do you?"

"No, sir . . ."

Rizzo picked up the book and flipped it open to a place he'd marked. He stared at the page, his lips pulling in against his teeth. He turned the book around, placed it in front of me, then pointed to a handwritten entry in the upper corner.

"Now why in god's name would you write something like that in this poor girl's autograph book?"

I leaned forward and looked. As soon as I saw it, I understood why Rizzo was so mad. In scraggly letters, someone had written: "Althea—You're a really nice girl, for a nigger. Have a great summer!"

West Lab had only integrated a couple of years earlier, in the fall of 1968. But there hadn't been any notable racial tension in school, even after the riots that broke out in Miami that initial year in the wake of Martin Luther King's assassination.

"Althea" was Althea Martin, one of the first black students to enroll.

I didn't know what to say. I knew I hadn't written the racist inscription—knew that it was a word my parents had taught us to revile. But even as an eleven-year-old I knew it would sound pathetic to try to use my liberal bona fides as a defense: "But my parents are old-school lefties—they cried when Dr. King was murdered . . . my nanny is a black woman . . . my idol is Muhammad Ali . . . and don't you remember my poem: 'Black and White, Yellow and Red / If we don't stick together we'll all be dead'?"

So I just said, "I didn't write that."

"Of course you did."

Oh, boy—here we go again. "No, sir . . . I didn't."

Rizzo suddenly exploded, springing from his chair and leaning across the desk.

"Cut the crap, son! We know you wrote this . . . so you might as well come clean!"

I was terrified. For a moment, I thought he might slap me. But with the words catching in my throat, I somehow mustered the wherewithal to push back: "What makes you so sure?"

Gathering himself, Rizzo sat back in his chair, and smiled. "It's very simple: that disgusting message was written with the same ink, and in the same handwriting, as your signature on the previous page." He flipped to the signature and grinned, eyeing me like Perry Mason, triumphantly waiting for the inevitable witness stand breakdown-and-confession.

I looked down and immediately realized what had happened. The signature belonged to a classmate whose first name also had three letters, and whose last name also began with an *S* (for legal reasons, I've been advised not to be any more specific).

"That's not my name," I said.

"Of course it is."

"No," I replied, growing indignant, "that's [*name withheld on advice of attorneys*]'s signature. I'm Roy Sekoff. *Sekoff*, not [*name withheld*]."

Rizzo turned his gaze to the signature. I saw his eyes narrow as it dawned on him that he had been accusing the wrong kid. He picked up the autograph book and gave it a closer look. He kept his eyes on the page for longer than necessary, then closed the book and put it back in his desk drawer.

I could see him trying to decide how to play this. He rubbed his hand over his mouth and stared at me. I did my best not to look too satisfied.

After a long pause, he just said, "You can go back to class now."

"That's it?" I asked incredulously.

"That's it."

It took every bit of inner discipline I possessed to not say: "Nice apology, asswipe!" But I held my tongue. *Who's lacking in self-control now, West Lab?!*

As I made my way back to class, my mind brimming with revenge fantasies—embarrassing lawsuit? stinging letter to the school board? banana in the tailpipe of his car?—I thought of *Billy Jack*. No, I couldn't whop Mr. Rizzo on the side of his face with my foot (even if I knew kung fu). But maybe I could get my classmates to line the halls and, in a show of defiance and support, raise their fists and bow their heads as I left the building: "One tin soldier rides away . . ."

I instantly realized that was never going to happen. So I settled for a solo reprise of Three Dog Night, howling at the top of my lungs: "Joy to the fishes in the deep blue sea / Joy to you and me . . ."

The words echoed down the empty corridor.

The Time Chevy Chase
Grabbed My Balls

The biggest laugh I ever got was the time Chevy Chase grabbed my balls. At a funeral.

(Okay, it was actually at a memorial service, but "funeral" sounds funnier.)

The year was 1994. The service was a boozy wake for comedy writer Michael O'Donoghue, legendary for his pitch-black contributions to *National Lampoon* and *Saturday Night Live*, who'd died of a cerebral hemorrhage at fifty-four years old.

I barely knew "Mr. Mike," but had had a brief yet memorable encounter with him a decade earlier.

I was working as the editor of *Laff Track*, a humor magazine that Scott, a college buddy of mine, had started. Our operating budget was extremely low—we sometimes paid writers, if we paid them at all, with bartered services like dry-cleaning, which we'd gotten in exchange for free ads. But our aspirations were high; we dreamed of being "our generation's *Lampoon*."

After publishing two well-received but barely seen issues, we'd run out of money. Now, a year later, buoyed by a small loan from Scott's father, we were ready to give it another go. And we were determined to make a splash.

Our miniscule staff gathered in our grungy offices near Hollywood and Vine to hash out ideas for our comeback issue. Since *Laff Track* was a freebie distributed at LA comedy clubs, record stores, and restaurants, we knew we needed an attention-grabbing cover that would compel people to pick up a copy—something like the classic *Lampoon* cover featuring a cute dog with a gun held to its head, and the words: "If You Don't Buy This Magazine, We'll Kill This Dog."

Our return issue would hit the stands in October 1983, so we began brainstorming edgy Halloween-themed concepts. The talk of *Lampoon* eventually landed us on O'Donoghue, whose dark, acid persona—including his famous *SNL* turn doing impressions of what acts like Tony Orlando and Dawn would sound like if they'd had long steel needles plunged into their eyes—seemed a perfect fit. What if we put O'Donoghue on the cover holding an apple with a bite taken out of it, exposing a bloody razor blade hidden inside?

Everyone was over-the-moon excited by the idea. The only problem was, we had absolutely no idea how to get ahold of O'Donoghue, let alone convince him to do the cover.

But we were all in our early twenties, hungry, and desperate—so a little thing like that wasn't going to stop us.

And it didn't.

Through a series of friend-of-a-friend-of-a-friend connections, we eventually tracked him down and were ecstatic to learn that he was currently in LA (clearly this was meant to be!), staying at Penny Marshall's house in the Hollywood Hills.

A few more calls scored us the number he could be reached at, and it was decided that Scott—whose greatest gifts as a publisher were his unwillingness to ever take "no" for an answer and the ability to deliver stem-winding motivational speeches (*you* try to get a writer to work for dry-cleaning coupons!)—would be the one to reach out.

Psyching himself up like a gladiator about to enter the Colosseum, Scott stepped into his office, closing the door behind him.

Soon enough, we could hear Scott's voice rising and falling, rising and falling. And although we couldn't make out the words, it was clear he was at his pleading, cajoling, gossamer-dream-spinning best. Then silence.

A moment later, Scott stepped out of his office, a look of beatific bewilderment on his face.

"He's going to do it," he said, not quite believing it himself. "He's going to do it!! And I convinced him to write an original story for us. We're doing the photo shoot the day after tomorrow."

Hugs and high fives ensued, and, two days later, a small group of us were in my car, making our way up a winding hillside road to "Penny's place." Joining Scott and me were Sam, our gifted but frequently volatile art director, and a freelance photographer named Wayne Williams, which struck us as especially apropos to the task at hand, since a man with that name had recently been identified as the serial killer responsible for the infamous Atlanta Child Murders.

I'm not sure what we were expecting to find—a crazed madman writhing on the floor, clutching at his punctured eyeballs, or a creep saying things like "I would like to feed your fingertips to the wolverines" (a line from the first-ever *SNL* sketch)—but the guy who greeted us at the door was thin-bordering-on-frail, soft-spoken, and reticent.

The first crack in his dour demeanor came when we introduced our photographer as "Not the child-killing Wayne Williams." He seemed to get a kick out of that.

While Wayne set up his lights, Scott, Sam, and I explained the razor-in-the apple concept. O'Donoghue nodded, took a puff on the long brown More cigarette he was smoking, then turned on his heels and walked out of the room.

Sam and I exchanged a worried glance—had we blown the whole deal? O'Donoghue returned a moment later wearing a wide-brimmed fedora and mirrored sunglasses.

"This should work," he said softly, taking his position in front of the camera.

Sam handed him the razor-laced apple we'd brought along, and Wayne began taking pictures, each shot punctuated by a pop and a flash. After a series of these, Wayne pulled us aside—he was worried that the razor blade was too subtle and wasn't "reading" as we'd envisioned.

We apprehensively shared Wayne's concerns with O'Donoghue, who again wordlessly turned on his heels and walked out of the room, this time in the direction of the kitchen.

When he came back, he was carrying the biggest, scariest-looking carving knife I'd ever seen.

"Let's try this."

Sam quickly adjusted the lights so they were aiming up at O'Donoghue, who brandished the knife next to his face. Wayne fired off a new round of pics.

"Okay, that should do it," said Mr. Mike, and we knew that it was time to go (or at least that he was done with us).

As we packed up our stuff, I heard Scott gingerly remind O'Donoghue of our deadline for the story he'd agreed to write. He just lit another brown cigarette and stared out the window at the city below (at least I think he was staring at the city below; it was hard to tell through the mirrored shades).

That night, we all gathered around as Wayne showed us the freshly developed contact sheets containing thumbnail versions of all the photos he'd taken. Rendered in stark, shadowy black and white, the images were riveting.

One picture in particular jumped out at us. O'Donoghue is holding up the knife, an impassive expression on his face. Due to the up-lighting, the brim of his fedora glows like a halo; the lenses of his sunglasses, catching the reflection of the lights, are filled with luminous triangles; and the massive knife shimmers ominously to the side. All against a crisp black background.

It was stunning. We knew we had our cover. (It's worth noting, fifteen years after appearing on the cover of *Laff Track*, that same photo was used on the cover of a bestselling biography of O'Donoghue, and, as of this writing, some thirty-four years later, it is the image that adorns O'Donoghue's Wikipedia page.)

What we *didn't* have was the promised story. And the deadline was rapidly approaching. Call after call went unanswered, voice messages went unreturned. When Scott finally managed to reach O'Donoghue, his pent-up frustration got the better of him: "It needs to be here soon, dammit!" he barked. Scott's frustration turned to dread as he took the phone away from his ear and stared at it, crestfallen. "He hung up on me! Can you believe it?"

Yes, we could. A consensus quickly formed: we were fucked.

While the rest of us desperately weighed our admittedly limited options, Vander Cecil, our associate publisher/ad director, an eccentric southerner prone to hard drinking and using the I-Ching to generate potential sales leads, decided that he was going to somehow "channel" O'Donoghue's spirit and write a piece we could pass off as the writer's.

Later that night, we found him in the office men's room, smelling of bourbon, staring deeply into the mirror, holding a knife and repeatedly telling his reflection: "I am O'Donoghue, I *am* O'Donoghue!" The pressure had clearly driven him over the edge, but none of us were about to say that to a knife-wielding drunk. We left him to his incantations.

The next morning, as we were resigning ourselves to the amateur-hour reality of running an O'Donoghue cover with no O'Donoghue story inside, and just hours before the final layout had to be delivered to the printer, a messenger strolled into our office and nonchalantly handed us an envelope containing "The Sparkle on the Knife"—a brief, wholly original spew that served as Mr. Mike's of-the-moment comedy manifesto. It read, in part:

> 1983. It's getting harder to find the veins. Time for the new Stalk 'n' Slash Humor. What sane man has not wanted to nail David Hartman's tongue to the floor? Or pound one hundred finishing brads into Bonnie Franklin's skull? Did I say "*one* hundred? I meant "*nine* hundred," of course. Who among us has not wondered if Shari Lewis and Lambchop will be buried in separate graves?
>
> The new Stalk 'n' Slash Humor. What's down in the well will come up in the bucket. Investigators find funnybones in landfills and crawl spaces. A gun in the mouth in a lampshade on the head. Punchlines are landing below the

belt. It's no longer enough to tickle the ribs. Now you must drive an icepick into the brain pan. Did I say *"an* icepick?" I meant *"nine hundred* icepicks," of course.

Classic O'Donoghue. Manna from Comedy Heaven. Perfect for *Laff Track.*

At that moment, you could've announced that a nuclear bomb was about to detonate in the middle of our offices, and not a single one of us would've either ducked or covered. We felt that indestructible.

Laff Track Issue Number 3 was soon rolling off the printing presses—and the O'Donoghue cover, rendered in our oversized format, was even more arresting than we'd hoped, simultaneously sinister and seductive.

The next morning, I trekked into the Hollywood Hills to take O'Donoghue a stack of copies. He was as enigmatic as ever, but seemed pleased. So I asked if he'd sign a copy for me. Agreeing, he picked up a black Sharpie and signed the cover, adding a message along the vertical edge of the menacing knife: "For Roy . . . Kiss Me. I'm Dead."

And now, eleven years later, he actually was.

A notice in the show-business trade papers said that a memorial service would be held that weekend at the Formosa Cafe, which had been a Hollywood hangout since the 1920s.

A few of us former *Laff Track* staffers decided it might be fun to go and bring along some copies of Issue Number 3. Since we'd printed less than ten thousand, we doubted most people had seen it, or ever read "The Sparkle on the Knife." Besides, it would be a good excuse to get the old band back together.

When we walked into the seen-better-days place, it was crowded and buzzing with chatter. Feeling a bit like interlopers, we stuck to the fringes of the room, quickly noticing a few faces only comedy nerds would recognize—including storied *National Lampoon* publisher Matty Simmons, and Anne Beatts who, along with being the first female editor of *Lampoon* and a standout writer during the early years of *SNL*, had once been O'Donoghue's girlfriend. We also spotted Chevy Chase holding court at the end of the bar.

After a bit of mixing and mingling, everyone moved into a back room for a round of toasts. One by one, Mr. Mike's friends and colleagues stood to offer their memories and tributes—a heartfelt mix of humor, profanity, and sorrow.

At one point, Chase moved to the center of the room and delivered a meandering monologue that was light on humor and heavy on Chevy. I noticed a lot of pursed lips and rolled eyes in the crowd. O'Donoghue's antipathy toward *SNL*'s first breakout performer was well known, but that didn't stop Chevy from taking his star turn before returning to his seat.

After everyone who wanted to speak had done so, I somewhat sheepishly made my way to the front, holding a *Laff Track*.

"Unlike almost all of you," I began, "I didn't know Michael very well. But over a decade ago, we put him on the cover of our magazine." I held up the issue. "And he wrote this really cool piece for us that I thought you might like to hear."

Just then, I became aware of a rustling off to my left. It was Chevy Chase.

"Excuse me," he said loudly. "Sorry to interrupt. But I've got to be going."

Taken aback, I stopped speaking and watched as he struggled to extricate himself from the booth he'd been sitting in and make his way toward the exit, a route that forced him to pass in front of me. As he did, he paused and offered me his hand. But as I went in for the handshake, he abruptly reached down and grabbed me by the crotch, his sizable mitt encasing the full three-piece set.

Utterly flummoxed, I didn't pull back.

"Nice balls!" he bellowed. And with that, he headed toward the door.

I stood there for a moment, not really believing what had just happened.

I glanced at the gathered faces; to a person they all seemed horrified or disgusted or filled with pity.

Just as Chevy was about to leave the room, my brain snapped back to life. I looked down at my crotch, smiled, and referencing Chevy's latest movie, which had recently opened to less-than-stellar reviews, said: "Wow. Alright then . . . Y'know, maybe *Cops and Robbersons* didn't suck as bad as I thought."

The room exploded with laughter. And I'm not talking about a polite guffaw or chuckle. I'm talking howling, shrieking, thunderous laughter. Wave after wave of it. I noticed Anne Beatts pounding the table with her palm. You know the scene in *All That Jazz* where Roy Scheider-as-Joe-Gideon is leading a table read for his new show, and everyone is roaring with laughter, their faces contorted in over-the-top hilarity? This was like that. Times ten.

Don't get me wrong; I realize that my retort wasn't actually all that funny—or even made sense. But because of the timing, the delivery, and the dynamic at play—a snappy comeback from the poor young magazine guy who'd just had his cock and balls manhandled by the pompous, bombastic movie star—the response was combustible.

I saw Chevy hesitate at the exit as the laughter passed over him like the shock waves from a roadside IED. He obviously knew something had been said, and that it likely was about him. But he didn't turn back; he just headed out the door.

When the laughter finally subsided, I looked at the crowd and picked up right when I'd left off: "Any-way . . . I thought you might like to hear the story Michael wrote."

Later, after everyone had moved back to the bar area, people kept coming up to me, shaking my hand and patting me on the back, with many of them commending me on my "great bit" (as if I'd written and rehearsed the whole exchange). Someone, I think it was either Anne Beatts or Matty Simmons, told me: "Michael always enjoyed shitting on Chevy. He would've loved that moment."

At one point, a young director approached me and asked if I had a script he could read. I asked him, "Are you really networking at a memorial service?"—then quickly assured him that I had an original comedy screenplay just outside in the trunk of my car.

I drove home giddily. Buzzing from the experience.

When my wife asked me how it had gone, I shrugged and told her: "What can I say? I killed at the funeral."

A coda:

In 2008, fourteen years after Chevy Chase grabbed my balls, I unexpectedly crossed paths with him again. It was at that year's

Democratic National Convention, in Denver. I was now the founding editor of the Huffington Post, which was hosting a big star-studded luncheon at the historic Brown Palace Hotel. After helping coordinate a panel discussion that featured Arianna, will.i.am, George Stephanopoulos, and Rahm Emanuel, it was time to eat.

The caterer told me there was an unoccupied seat at table thirty-six. As I approached the table, I saw that the chair next to mine was occupied by Chevy Chase. Taking my seat, I wondered what I should do: Should I remind him of the awkward incident? Seek retribution by "accidentally" spilling a glass of wine in his lap? Tell our table mates: "This jerk once grabbed my balls"?

I gave him a quick once-over. This was not the lean, lithe, youthful Chevy from Weekend Update, or the handsome, Cary Grant–lite rascal from *Foul Play* or *Caddyshack*, or even Clark Griswold Chevy, a dad who you could, if you squinted a little, accept Christie Brinkley flirting with—but never fucking. This wasn't even the stiff-as-a-board middle-aged Chevy who flop-sweated his way through his canceled-in-five-weeks talk show on Fox. This was sixty-five-year-old, Social Security Chevy—bloated, balding, and unmistakably on the downside of his career. A guy whose reputation as a first-class putz had turned his name into showbiz shorthand for "arrogant asshole." Not surprisingly, he looked miserable.

I decided not to say anything. It was more than enough for me to know that, to borrow a phrase, he was Chevy Chase . . . and I was not.

The Way of the Cow

By the middle of my junior year of college, I knew I wanted to get out as quickly as possible.

I'd always been a good but indifferent student. My greatest academic gifts were strong writing skills, an exceptional memory, and a well-honed talent for sucking up to teachers and administrators.

I had mastered the art of just barely clearing whatever scholastic bar was set in front of me, never pushing myself one millimeter higher than needed.

One of my favorite teachers, a literature professor who'd had some success as a novelist twenty-five years earlier, perfectly summed up my approach one day as he and I were strolling across campus after class, as we often did (see above re sucking up).

"You know you're not fooling me, don't you, Sekoff?" he said, pursing his lips.

"How so, Professor?"

"Well, let's look at you and Rybarczyk," he said, referring to a bright-eyed honors student taking the same Henry James seminar as me. "You only know half as much about *Portrait of a Lady* as she does. But on the last test, you were able to utilize one hundred percent of the fifty percent you knew; Rybarczyk was able to use fifty percent of the one hundred percent *she* knew. So you will both get the same grade. But you're not fooling me."

That, in a nutshell, was Roy Sekoff, college student.

Once I'd decided I wanted to graduate early, I knew I'd have to attend classes over the summer, then take a massive load in the fall (as well as search the official Student Handbook for any additional angles to be played).

That's how I found myself spending my summer Monday, Wednesday, and Friday afternoons in an honors philosophy class on existentialism.

We were two weeks into our six-week session, and the professor, George Weaver, a tall, lanky, balding, straightlaced man in his early fifties, was at the blackboard, writing out bullet points on the Nietzsche lecture he was giving.

All at once, he froze in midsentence, his arm still raised, elbow cocked, chalk in hand. He stood there for another moment, then lowered his head.

The class exchanged confused glances. Was he thinking? Suppressing a gurgle of acid reflux? Having a mild stroke?

He began to speak again, softly at first, then with rising intensity:

"This . . . is . . . bull . . . SHIT!!" Upon delivering that last shouted syllable, he whirled around to face the class and flung the piece of chalk he'd been using across the room; it exploded against the back wall.

We sat there, disbelieving.

He looked us over calmly, then pointed to the words he'd just been writing.

"This . . . is . . . bullshit." He made a sweeping two-armed gesture encompassing the entire room. "All of it. Bullshit."

We all stared at him blankly, not sure what the proper response was. Should we run for the door? Ask him to be more specific? See if there would be a quiz on this tomorrow—and, if so, whether it would be true/false or multiple choice?

Leaning back against a lectern, he rubbed his hand across his brow and shook his head. His eyes welled up with tears.

"You wanna know what's *not* bullshit?" he said, his voice choked with feeling. *(Indeed we do!)* "Love. Love's not bullshit . . . And passion is not bullshit . . . And confusion is not bullshit either . . ." He was picking up momentum, the words starting to rapidly tumble forth. "And desire isn't bullshit . . . And outrage . . . And sex. Sex isn't fucking bullshit, for sure! And that includes jerking off!"

A tear rolled down each of his now-flushed cheeks, his gaze flitting across our upturned faces.

"They want us to quiz you on Kierkegaard, but we should be quizzing you on your spirit, on your instincts, on your libido."

So there will *be a test on this tomorrow . . . ?*

He glanced out the window, seeming to slip into a reverie.

"When I was fifteen, there was a girl who lived across the street from me. She was fourteen and she was perfect and I loved her and I think she loved me. I wanted to have sex with her, but all we ever did was kiss—because that's what the world told her was allowed. I would've been fine with dry humping; I would've been fine with a hand job . . ."

Okay, so we'd gone from Heidegger to hand jobs. This was either the most unorthodox way of explaining existentialism in the history of education or Professor Weaver was on the road to Crazy Town.

The heaving, gut-wrenching sobs that soon filled the air provided the answer: this guy was flat-out losing his shit.

We all exchanged bewildered glances. The class syllabus hadn't said anything about nervous breakdowns. Not knowing what else to do, people slowly gathered their things and began to leave the room. A couple of philosophy majors who always sat in the front row hesitantly approached him; one began to reach for his shoulder but pulled back when he looked up.

"I'm sorry," he said. "I'm sorry . . ." He moved behind his desk and sat down, burying his head in his arm. He resumed sobbing. The rest of us silently walked out.

Now, if this happened today, Professor Weaver's rant would've been taped and gone viral before his fourth "bullshit." And half the class would've sprinted to the dean's office to report him for saying "hand job" without first providing a trigger warning.

But this was 1979, and those of us who gathered in the quad after his meltdown were mostly focused on whether whoever took over the class would be harder or easier than Weaver— while a few of us were fixated on what, exactly, a "libido quiz" would look like, and if it would be graded on a curve. One thing we all agreed on: that was the last we'd be seeing of Ol' George for a while.

Which is why when the next class session rolled around we were stunned to find Professor Weaver in his familiar spot at the front of the room. Only instead of his usual outfit of light blue button-down oxford shirt, tan slacks, tan socks, and tasselled loafers, he was wearing a tie-dyed tank top, cutoff shorts, and sandals. And he was holding two bags of oranges. A big grin lit up his face.

"Let's take a walk. Leave your books . . ."

Everyone was confused—and a little concerned. Why was he dressed like that? What were the oranges for? And was that a happy smile or the psychotic grin of a would-be ax murderer? But any fears we might have felt were outweighed by the collective realization that "leave your books" likely meant we wouldn't be spending the next ninety minutes dissecting Dostoyevsky. Anything to ditch a class!

So off we went, embarking on a leisurely stroll through the school grounds before settling under a shady tree by the edge of Lake Osceola, the murky man-made lagoon in the middle of campus. Since this was Miami in July, most of us were covered in sweat. (To understand what Miami in July feels like, go to your local health club, ask to see their steam room, step inside. Bingo.)

Professor Weaver passed out oranges and, as he peeled the skin off his, began to speak, his entire being radiating a calm usually only seen in meditating monks and heavily medicated schizophrenics.

"A couple of months ago I began seeing a therapist," he began. "He's a Reichian, specializes in what they sometimes call Orgone therapy. A couple of times a week, I go to his office and we work on prying off the layers of armoring I've covered myself with over the years. Sometimes it involves me getting on my knees and punching his couch while I scream at the top of my lungs . . ."

He was saying this in the most matter-of-fact manner possible.

"It brings up a lot of feelings—jealousy, guilt, shame. And a lot of memories I haven't thought about for a very long time."

"Like the fourteen-year-old they wouldn't let you screw?" said a brown-nosing student-government type who was always the first to raise his hand.

Weaver just nodded his head. "Yes, like her . . ." He seemed to be picturing her in his mind.

This was quickly shifting from eccentric to unsettling. But it was utterly mesmerizing.

Sensually biting into an orange slice, he dabbed a trickle of juice with the back of his hand, and continued.

"Now, and this is important, I want to talk to you about a new theory I've been working on. I call it the Way of the KOWW."

"The Tao?" asked the brown-noser.

"No, the KOWW."

"Cow? Like milk and moo?"

"No. It's K-O-W-W. It stands for the Killers of Worldly Wisdom."

"Should we be taking notes?"

"No, just listen. The Killers of Worldly Wisdom are the people who take the true, beautiful, pure souls we are all born with and suffocate them and crush them. They are the parents and teachers and priests and politicians who replace emotion with embarrassment, joy with humiliation, passion with guilt, love with shame. They are the ones who tell us 'no,' 'don't,' 'that's wrong,' 'you'll go to hell' . . . 'what will the neighbors think?' I say, fuck the neighbors! I care what *I* think . . ."

The tears returned to his eyes. Another orange slice. "Let's talk about the KOWWs . . ."

And that's exactly what we did every Monday, Wednesday, and Friday for the next three weeks.

We'd follow as Weaver strolled around campus, eating fruit and expounding on the Ways of the KOWW—and what we could do to counteract them. With regular detours down the road of his Reich-fired psyche, usually involving subjugated sexual desires and carnal regrets.

With his sandals, serene demeanor, and otherworldly pronouncements, he was like a crazy horny-but-repressed Jesus, and we were his perspiring disciples.

There was no homework, no books, no additional reading, no pop quizzes. While the rest of the summer student body was studying for finals, we were trying to figure out if he would give us all As or A-plusses.

It was too good to last.

And it didn't. On the last day of the semester, we showed up to class and were flabbergasted to find not Crazy Jesus Weaver standing at the front of the room but Button-Down Oxford and Tasselled Loafers Weaver—although we did notice that he wasn't wearing socks.

What the hell was going on? We looked around the room, convinced that we'd spot the aliens who had plonked this pod person into our midst, or the head of the Philosophy Department who'd finally told him to cut the KOWW shit or lose his tenure.

But there was no one in the room but the professor and his students. Weaver calmly indicated that we should take our seats and, without even the slightest mention of Reich or oranges or teenage hand jobs, proceeded to hand out our final exam.

It was in two parts, each worth fifty points. Part One consisted of twenty-five questions requiring short answers, based on material culled from the first two weeks of class (you could almost hear Kierkegaard, Nietzsche, Heidegger, and Sartre calling out: *Yeah, we back, bitches!*). Part Two was a single question: Tell me about a Killer of Worldly Wisdom from Your Life.

At first, no one but the brown-noser began taking the test. The rest of us just sat there, convinced we were the victims of the strangest *Candid Camera* prank in history. Or some sick existentialist joke. What about our spirits and our instincts? What about our libidos? But, one by one, my dumbfounded classmates all began answering the questions.

Every fiber of my being told me I shouldn't cave, that maybe this was the ultimate test of what he'd been teaching, that I should give the same answer to each of the Part One questions: "This . . . Is . . . Bullshit!" And make Tasselled Loafer George the subject of my Part Two KOWW essay.

That was the rebel move. The Orgone play. The ultimate WWCJW (What Would Crazy Jesus Write) stance.

But I really wanted to graduate early. So, using 100 percent of the 50 percent I knew, I answered the questions and turned in the test. I got an A and chalked up three more credits.

But I knew I wasn't fooling anybody.

The Book-Buying Trip

For most Jewish boys, being bar mitzvahed is the rite of passage into adulthood.

For the sons of Arthur Sekoff, it was being given the chance to tag along on his annual business trip to Nebraska, Illinois, and New York. My invite came in the summer of 1974, just as I was about to turn fifteen.

My father was the proprietor of Book Horizons, an independent college bookstore located across the street from the main entrance of the University of Miami, in Coral Gables, Florida. "Serving UM since 1953!"

For twenty-one years, Book Horizons had been the "friendly competition" to the school's "official" bookstore. It built its reputation on fast, personalized, bordering-on-overaggressive service—seconds after entering the compact, hadn't-been-redecorated-in-years store, a customer would be pounced on by a horde of workers chirpily asking, "May I help you?!" We prided ourselves on getting students in and out the door as quickly as humanly possible, fully loaded with their books, study aids, pens, pencils, notebooks, backpacks, and UM-branded T-shirts, shorts, sweatshirts, caps, key chains, and bumper stickers.

The store's other lure was its extensive collection of used books—"Used books can save you 25%, 50%, or even more!" Along with being cheaper for the customer, used books were a cash cow for the business. At the end of each school term, my dad would "buy back" a student's books, then resell that same book at a good-but-fair markup the following semester—the catch being whether the same course and books were still being offered.

The key to success was finding this out in a timely manner (often achieved by plying university employees with an after-work martini), then selling the ones that were "discontinued" to other college bookstores or wholesale distributors.

Over the years, my dad had become a virtuoso at playing this game. As part of the process, a couple of times a year buyers from the nation's three largest book wholesalers—Nebraska Book Company, Follett, and Barnes & Noble—would come to our store and buy up parts of the inventory we weren't planning to keep. To a man, these buyers were genial, glad-handing guys who smelled of Brylcreem, aftershave, and the hint of a lunchtime cocktail. Most summers my dad would make a book-buying trip to Lincoln, Chicago, and Manhattan, home to the Big Three. It wasn't necessarily an essential part of the business, but was useful in maintaining good relations.

And this was my year to accompany him.

The excursion wasn't gratis. As part of the bargain, I was slated to work full-time at the bookstore that summer.

My dad liked to say that "Book Horizons employs the unemployable." The ever-changing staff was a motley collection of students, relatives, musicians, former hippies, lost souls, and random people who wandered in off the street.

Now I was joining their illustrious ranks.

As a family member, I had worked at the store for years during "the Season"—the insanely hectic few weeks right before and after the start of classes each semester. This was when 90 percent of the bookstore's money was made; the rest of the year was spent getting ready—putting price tags on books, stocking shelves, and reordering in-demand T-shirts. In the early '70s, our "Sun Tan U" design was a big seller.

In my time there, I had graduated from "shelf restocker" to "book bagger" to "working the floor"—a prime position that involved getting students the books and supplies they needed in a "fast and friendly" manner. A key perk of this role was the accompanying face-to-face interaction with young, often very attractive coeds. When a good-looking girl would walk through the door, the competition among the floor workers to be the first to greet her with a smiling "May I help you?" was cutthroat. Bruised ribs were a common occupational hazard of the job.

And at this, the tail end of my fourteenth year of life, I was definitely a sexual force to be reckoned with: scrawny, short for my age, experiencing the preliminary stages of acne, with once-silky hair that, upon the arrival of puberty, had become a coarse tangle. It didn't help that, while attending an inner-city junior high, I had taken to using an Afro pick to "comb" it. But no one in my life had the compassion or decency to say the thing I most needed to hear: *"Conditioner!!"*

So there was not a lot of action with the coeds—or even girls my own age.

Which isn't to say that my hormones weren't raging. Puberty had hit me like a Dick Butkus blindside. Aided by purloined copies of my dad's fairly extensive collection of girlie mags and the stash of Super 8 stag films I'd "stumbled upon" during an exhaustive search of his closet, I was in a near-constant state of arousal. But doing something about it was usually fraught with anxiety and tension, since my bedroom was connected to a bathroom that I shared with my younger brother, with doors that only locked from the inside. The Great Leap Forward of simply jerking off in the shower was still six months from occurring to me.

When it came to the brave new world of sex, I was book smart, but with zero real-world experience. The closest I'd come to seeing a naked woman in person was when I accidentally walked in on my friend Benny Wooster's withered grandmother while she was peeling off a wet bathing suit. It wasn't a pretty picture—not that that stopped me from later pleasuring myself to the memory. Erotic beggars can't be choosers.

Growing up, I'd always idolized my father—a brilliant, boisterous, jocular contrarian whose personality would fill up any room he entered. He came by his nickname—"the Big A"— legitimately. He ruled the aisles of Book Horizons the way Vince Lombardi ruled the sidelines of the NFL. But he was way hipper than Vince. I always got the sense that he was somehow in the know, privy to the inside scoop, willing to push the bounds of tradition and propriety. He dug Lenny Bruce, adored Billie Holiday, campaigned for Henry Wallace, and easily rode the counterculture wave of the '60s.

Not that he didn't also scare me a little. He was a strong, stocky man—what my grandfather, Papa Sam, would call a "*shtarker*" in Yiddish. "Wait until your father gets home!" was a maternal threat my brothers and I took very seriously. "I could break you in two with one hand," Dad would casually remind us; and we had no doubt that he could.

At the time of the buying trip, he was fifty-two years old, but he didn't seem middle-aged to me. Maybe it's because his standard uniform at work was a T-shirt, walking shorts, and sneakers. It's hard to grow old in that outfit.

Despite my deep admiration for him, and his unmistakable affection for his children, it's not like we were particularly chummy with each other.

When I was a kid, he was more focused on work than child-rearing. He occasionally took my brothers and me on outings, but usually only to places he wanted to go: a Miami Dolphins game, a car ride to Miami Beach to visit his parents, out to dinner.

I can recall him actually playing with us very rarely: an occasional game of ping-pong in the garage or eight-ball on the pool table he'd bought for the "family room"; a single—thus very memorable—instance when, arriving home after work, he "stole" the basketball I was dribbling in the driveway and unleashed a two-handed set shot. It clanked off the rim.

So I was genuinely excited about the upcoming father-son trip. It would be a rare opportunity to spend time alone with him, without my mom or either of my brothers around.

Our first stop was Lincoln, Nebraska, where we met up with Nebraska Book Company rep Fred Sullivan, a ruddy-faced Irishman who would look completely at home if cast as an NYPD patrolman walking the beat and rousting *West Side Story* wannabes from in front of the corner store.

Before we toured the cavernous warehouse, Fred shook my hand and patted my back. I'm sure he would've tousled my hair if it wasn't already a rat's nest. Again I ask: Why had no one ever told me, "Conditioner, Roy"? It would've been the grooming equivalent of the guy advising Dustin Hoffman in *The Graduate*: "Plastics."

The one lasting memory of this part of the trip is my dad asking Fred about "the Gold Room." Fred blanched, sputtered, hemmed and hawed, then sputtered some more—struggling mightily to change the subject. The Big A seemed to be enjoying his discomfort.

Later that night, as we were flying to Chicago, he filled me in. It seems that the last time Fred had been in Miami, my dad had taken him out for dinner, and the buyer had gotten pretty hammered and let it slip that the company had a special room where they kept the used books in the best condition, but that "we don't let Jews in the Gold Room." He obviously hadn't remembered what he'd said, and my dad, always one to tweak the nose of a good-natured anti-Semite, had savored watching him squirm.

Next up, Chicago, home of Follett. The buyer there was Tommy Troxell, a short, bald, cherub-faced fellow with a contagious, giggly laugh. The warehouse visit was a carbon copy of the Nebraska experience—without the subtle racism. Tons of books, handshakes, and fake punches to the ribs.

Things promised to get a lot more interesting that night when the Big A and I would be meeting Tommy Troxell at Mister Kelly's, the iconic nightclub on Rush Street.

I was thrilled to be getting a rare glimpse behind the adult curtain. My older brother and I had always been allowed to hang around whenever my parents threw a party or had friends over. But we were inevitably herded off to bed while the night was still young. We would sit in our room, listening to the vague rumble of party chatter, frequently punctuated by high-pitched shrieks and booming bursts of laughter, and wonder what the hell the grown-ups were up to.

Morning-after reports from the front lines would only serve to pique our curiosity and fuel our imaginations: the time a corpulent cousin had sat down on a glass table and fallen through—requiring a frantic drive to the emergency room. Or the moment, renowned among the children of those who'd been there, when a besotted college professor had made a bet that he'd be willing to stand up on a chair, drop his pants, and recite a soliloquy from Shakespeare (the specific play has been much disputed over the years). The chair was mounted, the pants were dropped, but before the monologue could be delivered, the prof's penis poked its way out of his boxers. Or so the legend had it.

But this was going to be live and in person, a front-row seat to adulthood.

The night did not disappoint. My dad and Tommy were both in high spirits. Strong drinks were tossed back, off-color jokes were told, filters were removed. Tommy was particularly uncensored, offering frequent muttered comments about the relative hump-worthiness of passing women (the timeless sexist classics "get a load of the ass on that one" and "did you catch the rack on her?" both made an appearance), and flirting with the astonishingly tolerant waitress.

His commentary on the night's performers was similarly unbridled. The opening act was a young, flamboyant Bruce Vilanch. Tommy's take: "probably a homo." The headliner was singer Lana Cantrell, a sultry-voiced Aussie with a Jane-Fonda-in-*Klute* shag haircut, wearing a slinky, glittery outfit. Tommy's take: "She's sexy, but I wonder if she's a lesbo." Homosexuality was clearly a major focal point for him.

The night ended with my dad leaving the waitress a very big tip ("Keep the change, sweetheart!"), and Tommy giving me a boozy bear hug before hopping in a cab. It was *Mad Men* come to life.

It felt like I'd matured five years over the course of five hours. And New York was still to come. Was it ever.

The Barnes & Noble portion of the schedule was uneventful—more books, banter, and boredom.

But the highlight of the entire trip was about to go down: a night at the theater. There was a lot to choose from on Broadway that summer. The original productions of *Grease, Pippin,* and *The Magic Show*; a widely praised revival of *Candide,* directed by Harold Prince; and an award-winning production of Eugene O'Neill's *A Moon for the Misbegotten,* starring Jason Robards and Colleen Dewhurst.

My dad decided to take me to see *Let My People Come,* a raunchy, rollicking production playing to packed houses at an off-Broadway theater in Greenwich Village. According to reviews, the self-proclaimed "sexual musical" made *Oh! Calcutta!* look like a Disney production.

As we picked up our tickets, Dad asked the young woman behind the box-office window, "Alright if this young fellow sees the show?" She eyed me carefully, an uneasy expression on her face, then broke into a broad smile. "Of course," she chirped. "What better way for him to learn, right?"

My father and I headed downstairs into the theater. It was a cabaret setting, with a small stage ringed by tables. We had excellent seats. We were soon joined by an attractive young couple. He was fair-haired and muscular; she was a buxom redhead. I had no doubt Tommy Troxell would've had something to say about "her rack."

Pleasantries were exchanged, then cut short as piano music started to play. All at once, the muscular guy sitting at our table stood up and started to take off his clothes. All of his clothes. He was promptly joined by the redhead. In short order, buck-naked men and women dotted the audience. They began to sing:

"I love to screw, with you. Any-where at all . . ."

Ho-ly fuck! For a kid who'd never seen a naked person in the flesh before, this was an overwhelming amount of flesh to take in. As the cast made its way onto the stage, the women continued:

"Grab my ass, step on the gas . . . Screw me to the wall!"

My eyes darted wildly about; there were boobs and butts and bushes of every size and shape. And a varied collection of penises too, though I tried hard not to look at *them.*

I also tried hard not to get hard—no easy task given my heaving hormones and the smorgasbord of heretofore concealed erogenous zones parading just a few feet away. A wave of panic washed over me: what if I got a boner that refused to heed my internal command to vacate the premises?

Onstage, the cast was grabbing and grinding each other, simulating a profusion of sex acts. And a thought popped into my head: How are the men not sporting major wood? Do they all engage in a pre-curtain circle jerk to defuse the situation?

I glanced at my dad, who appeared thoroughly engrossed in the lascivious proceedings.

The opening number gave way to a twangy country tune, with a sweet-faced actress singing, "I want a man who loves to fuck, who can keep it up for days . . . who can make me come a thousand different ways."

And so it went, salacious song after bawdy ballad, with titles like "I'm Gay," "Dirty Words," "Fellatio 101," and "Come in My Mouth."

A *New York Times* review of the show I read many years after the fact noted its "sweet, rather innocent messages about sex" and "surprisingly touching songs and sketches about intimacy, women's rights, gay life, lesbian love, all presented as fun, healthy, and just not that big a deal." But my viewing was much less nuanced; I found it hard to focus on anything other than the boobs, butts, bushes, and ballsacks. And the nipples; can't forget them.

The show ended with "Let My People Come," a rousing finale that, if you'll pardon the expression, climaxed with the full company onstage taking their curtain call in the buff. The crowd gave them a standing ovation—in my case, in more ways than one.

The cast then lined up in a receiving line reminiscent of a wedding, that is if the traditional bridal party was sweaty, out of breath, and unabashedly naked.

As my dad and I made our way down the line, shaking the performers' hands, my playbill being put to supplemental use as a codpiece, I tried my best to ogle but appear nonchalant. I kept my chin up, forcing myself to look into the eyes of each troupe member, and not at their members.

Many of them appeared to get a kick out of having a teenage boy see the show. I received a lot of grins, playful smirks, and loaded "Hope you liked its"—with plenty of knowing winks to my dad, who seemed pleased and proud of himself.

After purchasing me a cast album and commemorative T-shirt, Dad hailed a cab.

"So . . . what'd you think?" he asked as we slid into the back seat.

Part of me wanted to yell: *Well, I just stood three feet away from a naked woman with big pink nipples and a full bush singing about a guy coming in her mouth—what do you think I think?!*

Another part wondered if this might be a good opportunity to have an honest and open conversation about sex. We'd never had the Talk. Maybe this was my chance to ask one of the dozens of questions swirling around my head: "What's it feel like to get a blow job?" "How do you know if a woman has an orgasm?" "Is 'cunnilingus' the same thing as 'head'?"

Should I break down the wall and ask him if he actually realized—and, who knows, was even okay with—me dipping into his porn collection any chance I got? It would certainly save me from always having a side order of jitteriness with my titillation entree. Or maybe that was a smut bridge too far.

In the end, I just channeled Peter Brady: "It was far out!"

Back at the hotel, while Dad took a late shower, I tried to process the experience.

On the one hand, I'd obviously loved every sexy second of it. And I was delighted my dad thought I was mature enough for the adult content.

But was it weird that he took me there? Was the idea really, as the box-office lady said, to help me learn? Was this the musical-theater equivalent of a father taking his son to a whorehouse in Tijuana—only instead of watching a woman shoot a ping-pong ball out of her vagina, we got three-part harmony about sucking dick?

Or did we go because it was something *he* wanted to see? Was this part of the lure of the buying trip, a chance to be away from my mother and pursue his prurient predilections? And, if so, so what? It's not like he was Willy Loman and I was Biff, catching him with that woman in the Boston hotel room.

I heard the water in the bathroom cut off and I couldn't help but wonder if, turned on by the show, he'd decided to take a shower so he could employ the Great Leap Forward and toss one off in private.

That was definitely not something I wanted to think about. I literally tried to shake the image out of my head. The vision was replaced by the memory of the times, as kids, my older brother and I would shower with my dad—and I'd find myself face-to-face with what, to a five-year-old, must have seemed like a truly horrifying thing: a grown-up schlong covered in hair and intimidatingly bigger than mine. My brain shuddered again, then clicked on a more recent memory, from right around the time I was hitting puberty: as I slipped off my trunks after a swim, I noticed my dad taking a glimpse at my privates, obviously wanting to see if something—either hair or dick—was growing down there.

Paging Dr. Freud, paging Dr. Freud. Code Blue in Mr. Oedipus's room. Stat!!

When Dad stepped out of the bathroom, wearing boxers and a robe, I acted like I was drifting off to sleep.

"So, son, did the infamous Book Horizons buying trip live up to your expectations?" he asked.

"Oh, absolutely. It was a lot of fun . . . Unforgettable. Thanks."

He smiled and kissed me on the forehead.

"Good night, boychick."

"Good night, Dad."

He climbed into his bed and shut off the light. Even in the dark, I could tell he was smiling.

After a long pause, I heard him say:

"That was some show, huh?"

It sure was.

The Church of the High Colonic

For the first twenty-three years of my life, I never thought about sticking anything up my ass. At least not seriously. Then Tim became my roommate.

No, this isn't a story about my first homosexual experience. It's a story about my colon, coffee, rubber tubing, water siphoning, and how I went from a guy with a "bad stomach" to a fervent acolyte, and sometime evangelist, at the Church of the High Colonic—along with many of its offshoot sects, including (but not limited to) Fasting, Juicing, Food Combining, Vegetarianism, Raw Foodism, Homeopathy, and Chiropractic.

It was 1982, and I had just moved from Miami to Los Angeles to pursue my master's degree at USC's lauded film school, leaving behind my family, my friends, the most serious romance of my young life, and a regimen of psychotherapy that had, with my impending journey west, ballooned from every other Thursday to five times a week.

What I hadn't left behind was a crappy diet, a near-constant state of anxiety that tended to manifest itself as "digestive issues," and a subsequent obsession with my health—more specifically, the lack thereof.

I came by my "bad stomach"—and the anxiety—honestly. I was the second son of a hypochondriacal mother and a father who liked few things more than taking a good dump in the morning, with a smart and sensitive older brother who took to the family focus on the eliminative process like a prodigy.

My dad adhered to an unwavering morning ritual of a cup of coffee followed by a small, knowing grin, the stentorian announcement that it was time for his "morning ablutions," and a quick exit for the nearest bathroom, taking the Sports section of the paper with him. He'd reappear sometime later, his mood notably brighter, the paper somewhat worse for wear.

My mother was less predictable, often making a sudden, startling break for the bathroom in the middle of a sentence, tossing a hurried "gotta go!" over her shoulder as she raced off. She regularly complained of stomachaches, and would frequently expound on what made for, and where to find, the best public bathrooms. She was a big proponent of hotel lobby restrooms, but would accept a hospital lav in a pinch.

However, despite this poop-centric pedigree, for most of my childhood and teen years I never gave too much thought to what gastroenterologists professionally refer to as "going number two."

But I was certainly setting the foundation for my future troubles with a diet that featured lots of sugary cereals with milk, a steady stream of steaks and creamy desserts, an endless parade of chips, pretzels, crackers, and candy bars, frequent intake of fast-food, and a weekly dose of take-out Chinese food, including cartons of fried rice, fried egg rolls, and fried wontons (seeing a pattern there?).

And lots and lots of pizza. Starting in high school, I ate pizza almost daily. Whenever we ordered it, I'd always get an extra couple to put in the freezer so I could break off a frozen slice in the coming days to nuke in the microwave for a cheesy afternoon snack.

There was also a torrent of soda. Our garage was always stocked with a variety of sugary, carbonated beverages: Coke, Diet Coke, 7UP, ginger ale, root beer, Tab for my mom, and the odd can of Dr. Brown's Cream Soda for when my dad wanted a sip of nostalgia while downing a corned beef sandwich.

This devotion to soda persisted despite a memorable experience where, after my dad's Mercury station wagon broke down in the middle of central Florida during a family vacation, a toothless mechanic, seeing that a thick glob of accumulated grease was disrupting the prime functioning of the car, had poured a bottle of Coke over the engine. We watched as the gunk bubbled, fizzled, then quickly melted away. For some reason, we failed to mentally transfer that science fair–worthy demonstration of the corrosive power of the beverage over to the linings of our stomachs—and kept downing the stuff at a prodigious rate.

By the time I headed west for grad school, I was the picture of health. The "Before" picture. A person susceptible to frequent colds, sore throats, swollen glands, sinus congestion, headaches, and—like dear old mom—the sudden need to find a bathroom.

Enter Tim, a childhood friend who was moving to LA to try his hand at acting. Tim was energetic, quick to laugh, and independent in a host of ways that I wasn't. He knew how to cook, do his own laundry, and unclog a sink, and didn't consider screwing in a lightbulb a grand achievement in home repair.

He was also very good-looking, and had, while in high school, appeared in a number of national TV commercials, including one for Coke that required him to chug down an icy bottle of the syrupy liquid and smile like he'd just swallowed a mouthful of pure sunshine. This was no small feat—indeed, it required a level of acting rarely seen outside the Old Vic or a Meryl Streep movie—for Tim was what my father would lovingly call "a health nutjob."

He didn't smoke, drink alcohol or soda (except when being paid to do so), or eat red meat, and did his best to avoid refined sugar, dairy products, white flour, hydrogenated oils, processed foods, and the myriad additives and preservatives that have become so prevalent in our diet they deserve their own USDA food group.

Tim's health nutjobbery was hard-won. While we were in high school, he'd watched as his mother was ravaged by cancer; and, despite being one of the physically strongest people I'd ever met (the kind of guy who could do twenty-five pull-ups in the third grade), he'd fought his own battle against debilitating headaches and a painful skin condition—a state of affairs he eventually linked to his typically American (i.e., crappy) childhood diet, and years spent helping with his dad's exterminating business and the regular exposure to the toxic chemicals that came along with the gig. While our family's garage was well stocked with soda, his was filled with unsealed barrels of malathion, Dursban, chlordane, and DDT. And soda.

These youthful challenges ultimately set him on the path to studying alternate approaches to health and healing, a journey of trial and error that was in full swing when he moved in with me. The impact on my life—and my daily menu—was immediate: I began eating less junk and more fresh fruits and vegetables, which, I suddenly realized, could be lightly steamed and accented with a squirt of lemon instead of boiled within an inch of their life and drowned in a creamy sauce. White bread was traded for whole wheat, potato chips for rice cakes; and sodas were blacklisted, replaced by bottled juices.

But I had no idea the bizarre turn things were about to take.

The shift from dietary changes to voluntary starvation and anal invasion started with a visit from Tim's uncle Bob, whose teenage daughter had also died of cancer. In the process of trying to save her, he'd explored all kinds of alternative treatments and clinics—and had become convinced of the value of "body detoxification" through the use of prolonged fasting and the cleaning out of one's large intestines via so-called high colonics.

Over a dinner of stir-fried veggies and brown rice, Uncle Bob told us about a "cleansing program" he'd recently come across. Terms like "toxic colon," "chronic constipation," "putrefactive fecal material," and "intestinal flora" filled the air like a noxious gas. But my two main takeaways were that the program included going seven days without eating anything, and daily use of an apparatus that allowed you to self-administer a colonic in "the comfort and safety of your own home." Both of which struck me as things to be avoided at all cost.

That was when Uncle Bob whipped out the deal sealer: a sky-blue paperback with the poetic title *Tissue Cleansing Through Bowel Management*. This was the bible of colon cleansing, the magnum opus of "bowel consciousness" (the subject of Chapter One), the ultimate guide to literally getting your shit together.

It had detailed diagrams, step-by-step instructions, testimonials from patients who'd had their lives transformed by the seven-day fast/cleanse program, and, toward the back of the book, page after page of full-color photos of, as the book put it, "the shocking effluence" released by colonic flushing—"3 and 4 foot long ropes of hard-as-truck-tire-rubber material" that had accumulated inside people's large intestines.

All I could think was, *Ho-ly crap!*

Tim was all-in. He couldn't wait to order the whole colonic kit and caboodle, aka the Vit-Ra-Tox No. 59 Seven-Day Cleansing Kit, including the key item: the do-it-yourself at-home colonic unit, known as a Colema Board (part colonic, part enema—all evacuating!).

I was somewhat less enthusiastic. Yes, I certainly liked all the purported benefits of cleansing my colon: increased energy, improved mood, sharper mental clarity, better digestion, clearer and brighter skin, shinier hair, increased libido, lowered risk of colon cancer, and a supercharged immune system. But I just couldn't get my head around the seemingly impossible, potentially suicidal, idea of going without food for seven straight days. I'd never gone more than a few hours without eating; when I was a kid, I'd even had to sneak a snack in the temple bathroom during Yom Kippur services. I'd figured I could always atone for my apostasy the following year, kind of the rollover minutes of penitence.

And then there was that thing about sticking a tube up my ass and "irrigating" my colon with five gallons of water (spiked with coffee to help stimulate elimination). Call me unenlightened, but when it came to my Hershey Highway, the traffic was strictly one-way.

Uncle Bob countered that the beauty of the Colema Board was that the part that went inside you was so small—"thinner than a pencil"—you barely knew it was there, as opposed to the anus-stretching nozzle used by a traditional colonic hydrotherapist. His reassuring tone, coupled with Tim's rapturous enthusiasm—along with the unshakable images from the *Bowel Management* book of the tar-like stuff potentially lining the walls of my bowels—ultimately won me over, and I agreed to put up half the money for a board, and order my own Vit-Ra-Tox Seven-Day Cleansing Kit (with no intention of actually fasting or cleansing until some undetermined time in the distant future).

Like a pair of kids sending away for one of those mysterious treasures found in the back of comic books—"just add water" Sea-Monkeys, or X-Ray Spex that allowed you to "instantly see thru clothing"—we put our orders in the mail and went about our business. For me, this meant focusing on my upcoming film school final exams.

I got so immersed in this work, I completely forgot about my bowels—and any notion of cleaning them out.

So I was caught completely off guard when I came home one afternoon to find a big empty cardboard box ripped open in the middle of the living room floor and the overpowering smell of freshly brewed coffee filling the air. I quickly spotted a smaller box, this one sitting on the kitchen table. It was filled with bottles of Vit-Ra-Tox products. An unexpected wave of disappointment washed over me; wouldn't it have been cooler if the box contained Sea-Monkeys or X-Ray Spex? The sound of a toilet flushing snapped me back to reality.

Making my way through a fog of coffee fumes, I stopped outside the door to our apartment's only bathroom. "Hey, Tim, I'm home!"

"Cool, bro . . . I'm on the board. It's awesome!" Another flush rang out.

I'm not sure if it was a Pavlovian response to the flushing sound, or the fact that I'd just spent over an hour making my way from USC to our West LA apartment in rush-hour traffic, but I suddenly realized that I badly needed to take a leak.

"Uh, Tim, you got any idea how long you'll be in there?"

"Just started a little bit ago . . . it could be a while. I've got another three and a half gallons to go."

"Okay. Got it . . . Enjoy!"

My brain instantly raised my Bladder Alert level to DEFCON 2. I needed to figure something out—fast. I thought about going outside, but our apartment was surrounded by other apartments; there wasn't a secluded tree or bush anywhere in the vicinity. A dash to the nearest gas station, which wasn't all that near, seemed problematic at best, so I made an executive decision, hurriedly found a large mason jar, took up a position in a carpet-free corner of the living room (in case of unexpected overflow), and let it fly. This later became my go-to move whenever Tim was visiting Colonic Town.

By the time Tim emerged from the bathroom, his face flushed, his hair disheveled, and his eyes alight with the euphoric glow of the recently baptized, I was taking my first bite of a big bowl of pasta primavera. He looked at my food longingly.

"The board came right after you left this morning," he said. "I decided to dive right into the cleanse. I haven't eaten all day."

I glanced at my pasta, suddenly guilty. "Oh, sorry . . . I didn't know."

"Not a problem . . ."

He stepped into the kitchen and began preparing a concoction I soon came to know as the Cleansing Drink: 8 ounces of water; 1 tablespoon of bentonite (a clay suspended in water; "it acts like a sponge, mopping up undesirable debris"); 1 teaspoon of psyllium (a powder that turns into a mucilaginous gel); and 2 ounces of apple juice, all mixed together in a pint jar.

My heart skipping a beat, I did a double take to make sure he wasn't using the jar I'd just turned into my portable outhouse. Thankfully, it wasn't. I think.

Tim forcefully shook the jar, blending the ingredients, then quickly chugged it down. Wiping his mouth, he told me, "You gotta down it fast. The powder turns into a gel that makes its way undigested into the colon, softening and loosening any of that putrefactive gunk that might be sticking to the wall of your bowels. It's kinda nasty, but whatever . . ."

I took another bite of my pasta, somewhat less enthusiastically, as Tim continued his postcolonic spiel. "It was only my first one," he reported, "but I started to get some amazing stuff out by the end. There was one point where I'd let a lot of water in, made it all the way over to my ascending colon"—he pointed to a spot on his right side, just below his rib cage—"and I started to cramp really bad. Hurt like hell. But I kept massaging it, like the book says . . . and, all at once, *whoosh!*, everything released and I felt a bunch of stuff come flying out. It felt like the greatest dump of all time. And, god, was it foul!"

I twirled up another forkful of pasta, but my appetite was waning rapidly.

"Next time," said Tim, "I'm going to put a colander in the toilet to catch the stuff that's coming out, so I can see if it's like the black, rubbery crud in the pictures."

I nodded, putting down my still-loaded fork. Tim's stomach growled. "Damn, I'm hungry . . . that garlic smells fantastic." His stare burned a hole in my pasta bowl.

And, in that moment, I knew that I was going to cast aside caution—and millennia of human behavior—and willingly embark on the no-food/stuff-up-my ass journey. There was no way I was going to be able to go on like this for seven days, making a ravenous man watch me eat while being regaled with stories of the repulsive things pouring out of his butthole.

I made a modest proposal: if he could wait a week until I finished my finals, we could do the seven-day fast together. And since neither of us had enough money to go home for the holidays, we could make it a Christmas Cleanse and head into the new year with fresh attitudes and even fresher colons. Tim immediately agreed to chalk up his recent time on the board as a "practice colonic," and happily wolfed down the rest of my pasta.

One week later, the last of my finals completed, I returned home to once again find Tim in the bathroom, and the apartment smelling of coffee—but this time the familiar aroma was laced with a retch-inducing chemical stench. For a minute, I thought an exterminator had come by to fumigate the place while I was out.

Just then, Tim stepped out of the bathroom, wearing nothing but a pair of tighty-whitey underwear and heavy-duty rubber dishwashing gloves. Shaking his head, he let out a whoop.

"Damn, you smell that, bro?!" he asked.

"Uh, yeah . . . Kinda hard not to."

"That's all those pesticides I used to work with . . . they're finally leaving my body!"

Choking back a powerful urge to gag, I shrugged and said, "It's vile, but look on the bright side, there isn't a bug on the planet dumb enough to come within a mile of this place!"

We shared a boisterous laugh, and quickly opened all the windows—which, even though it was cold outside (okay, cold for LA), we kept open for the next seven days.

"What's with the gloves?" I asked.

Holding his hands up like a surgeon about to head into the OR, Tim said, "Dude, if we are going to be sharing the board, we're going to have to clean that mofo like it's Karen Silkwood going through the decontamination process! I'm just about done. So start loosening that sphincter, you're up next!" He patted me on the chest with the glove, and headed back into the bathroom.

After forcing myself to not think about where that glove had just been, I leaned out one of the open windows and took a deep breath. I understood there was no turning back now.

Before I knew it, I was standing in the bathroom, naked from the waist down, eyeing the setup in front of me: a four-foot-long board with a hole on one end, positioned over the toilet, the other end supported by a folding metal chair. There was a half-moon "splash guard" surrounding the back end of the opening, through which a thin plastic tip was protruding. The tip was connected to a long section of rubber tubing that led up to a five-gallon jug filled with water and a quart of coffee, which had been placed on a stool a few feet above the board, allowing suction and gravity to pull the water from the jug, through the tube, and into your (well, *my*) colon. A metal clip attached to the tubing allowed for control of when and how much water flowed in and out of you. The plastic tip (we each had our own) had been coated with K-Y Jelly, and I was supposed to lie down on the board and slide the tip into my bunghole.

Instead, I just stared at the setup and, for reasons I can't explain, wondered what Miss Jenny, my beloved preschool teacher, who had once discerned so much promise in me, would think if she could see me now. This thought tightened my ass even further, the opposite physical response than was currently called for.

"You on yet?"

It was Tim, who was standing on the other side of the bathroom door, generously ready to talk me through, as he warmly put it, "popping my colonic cherry."

"Just about," I replied.

I scrambled onto the board, positioning my supposed-to-be-an-exit-but-about-to-become-an-entry right against the tip. But I couldn't bring myself to take the next step. I just kept thinking about the notice on page 120 of the *Bowel Management* book: "USE GREAT CAUTION. Insert plastic tip no more than 3 inches past anus . . . pressing the tip in too far could result in perforation of the bowel wall." This process was clearly not designed for neurotics.

"Just relax your butthole and slide on," I heard Tim say. "Think of a flower opening up for a bee." Great, now a bee was going to fly into my ass and sting me. *Not the best metaphor, pal!*

Exhaling heavily, I thought flower—but not bee—and somehow, miraculously, I soon had the thing up my butt and hadn't perforated my colon. At least I didn't think I had.

"Okay, it's in!!" I exulted like a horny teen who, at long last, had finally "gone all the way."

And we were off. Tim patiently talked me through the process of letting a little water in, then expelling it whenever the urge hit. This is another of the highly desirable features of the Colema Board: the tip is so thin, the water and any fecal material it's carrying can easily slip around it. The goal is to get the water as far into your colon as possible—up the descending colon, across the transverse colon, and down the ascending colon (it's amazing how much I was learning about my intestines!)—but, truth be told, I was having a very hard time getting past my sigmoid colon, the last stop on the poop train before Rectum Station. I kept releasing the water soon after letting it in.

I was down to less than two gallons left in the jug before I finally relaxed enough to get a decent flow of water going. I could soon feel my belly puffing up, and the water sloshing around inside it. Then, as if someone had flipped an on/off switch, I suddenly couldn't get the water to come out. No matter how hard I tried, I couldn't seem to let go. I started to cramp. And panic. A wave of nausea washed over me. What was I supposed to do? What if I was stuck like that forever? (See above realization that this was a process clearly not designed for neurotics.)

Tim calmly reminded me to locate the source of the cramp and gently massage it. I did. Nothing. I tried again, pressing harder this time. Again nothing. I pressed harder still. Finally, after nearly rubbing the area raw, I felt it: a tiny shift. A miniscule moment of release. Like a freight train approaching in the distance, my belly began to rumble, the feeling growing more and more intense until, suddenly, my sphincter muscle relaxed, the gates at Rectum Station flew open, and . . . *whoosh!* A rush of water, coffee, and whatever the psyllium powder-turned-gel I'd been downing all day brought with it came flowing out of me, hitting the toilet bowl with a loud splash that clearly caught Tim's attention.

"Woo, bro . . . sounds like you got some results with that one!" he exclaimed from the other side of the door.

I just lay there a moment, feeling drained yet strangely accomplished. I was surprised to hear myself release a goofy giggle.

I soon emptied the jug, slid off the plastic tip, donned the rubber gloves, and went to town cleaning and disinfecting the board. A little wobbly, I stepped out of the bathroom into the cold, still-fetid air. Tim patted me on the back and rubbed my shoulder. "One day down, six more days to go!" he said. Whatever sense of accomplishment I'd felt rushed out of me faster than that last load of shit. Six more days of this? I didn't see how I could make it. I slowly trudged to the kitchen for my last Cleansing Drink of the day.

The next few days were a grind. I hadn't realized how involved "the program" was. No, we weren't eating, but five times a day we had to down our ten-ounce Cleansing Drink, featuring the psyllium and clay-water combo, which we started calling our "Silly-Yummy cocktail." At regular intervals, we'd also have to ingest an array of supplements and vitamins—38 pills every three hours, for a total of 162 a day. We got to where we could swallow fistfuls of pills at a time, but it got old in a hurry. Then there were the daily colonics, which, between the prep, the actual doing, and the industrial-strength cleanup, occupied a significant slice of the day.

The supplements and the sludgy Cleansing Drinks kept our bellies full, but did little to stop the hunger pangs. For the first few days, I found myself daydreaming of foods I hadn't eaten in years. Bagels and lox. A gooey Reuben sandwich. Frozen Klondike bars. I was like a pregnant woman from a '60s TV sitcom.

Then came Night Four. I was sitting on the couch, rereading the *Bowel Management* manifesto for the umpteenth time, trying my best not to breathe in the by-now-standard pesticide funk that accompanied one of Tim's colonics, when a cry rang out from the bathroom.

"Oh, my god!"

I hurried to the door, concerned. "You okay in there?"

"Oh my god!"

"Tim?"

A beat, and the door cracked open, unleashing a withering stink that almost dropped me to my knees.

"Dude, you gotta see this . . . ," he said.

74

He opened the door a little farther. More fetid air escaped. Through watering eyes, I could see that he was wearing the rubber gloves.

"You want me to come in? Now?"

"I know it's rank as fuck, but I gotta show you something."

He led me to the commode. Nestled within the toilet seat was a plastic colander, which held the collected detritus of his just-completed colonic. Slowly he reached down and, using two fingers, delicately held up a long, black rope of rubbery gunk, shaped like what I now knew a colon looked like. He beamed like a man brandishing the record-breaking bass he'd just hooked and landed.

"This just came out of me. Can you believe it? Isn't that disgusting?"

I immediately agreed that it was.

Placing the colon rope back into the colander, he picked up a plastic fork he'd obviously brought in for the occasion, and poked at the colonic refuse like it was a venomous snake.

"Look how hard it is . . . ," he said. He then picked up the colander and sloshed it around a bit, like a miner panning for gold. "I was really on a roll there, *whoosh* after *whoosh* after *whoosh*, when suddenly I sensed this sucker breaking loose. It felt like I was giving birth. When I got off the board and spotted this, I had to let you see it."

"I appreciate that."

"If you don't mind, I want to get some plastic wrap, and put it in the freezer," he said, nodding toward the colon-shaped junk.

I had no idea why he wanted to preserve it, or who he intended to show it to—a doctor? a future girlfriend? someone from the Smithsonian?—but I just nodded and said "Sure" (making a mental note to remember which side of the freezer he chose to use, just in case I ever decided to follow through on my Klondike-bar fantasies).

Let me take a moment here, if I may. Now, I fully recognize that this bit about the frozen turd thingy will probably sound incredibly bizarre to most normal folks. And looking back on it from a distance of multiple decades, it seems pretty bizarre to me as well. But, at the time, standing in a reeking bathroom, sifting through a colander full of rubbery ropes of bowel dregs, and discussing freezing some of it for posterity struck me as utterly normal. It's like how Scientologists don't blink an eye over the fact that their creation story involves a dictator named Xemu who seventy-five million years ago brought billions of people to earth in a spacecraft, stacked them around volcanoes, and killed them with hydrogen bombs. We were definitely hovering around the edges of Cultville. Jim Jones's followers drank the Kool-Aid; we drank the Silly-Yummy.

Over the course of our week-long cleanse, we continued to tweak and refine what we came to think of as "the colonic experience." We added a pillow for our heads to rest on, lit scented candles to set a mellower mood and combat the noxious smells, and made a colonic mixtape to listen to as we lay on the board. To this day, I can't hear Dan Fogelberg's "Longer," Bonnie Raitt's "I'm Blowin' Away," or the Police's "Roxanne" without feeling like I need to empty my bowels—a sense memory I'd forgotten about until I recently saw Sting in concert at the Hollywood Bowl (my apologies to anyone in Section J2, Row 13 whose toes I might have stepped on in my rush to make it to the men's room as soon as I heard those distinctive opening notes).

We plodded along to the end of Day Seven, a bit bedraggled, and skinnier than an abandoned dog in an ASPCA commercial. But after some 1,134 pills and countless gallons of Silly-Yummy, we finally were done, proud that we had completed "the mission."

A series of post-cleanse firsts followed. Our first food: shredded carrots, slightly wilted. Blazingly good. Who knew that wilted carrots could taste so delicious? A five-star Michelin meal was never as satisfying. And, of course, our first clean-colon-produced dump: simply remarkable.

I soon discovered that the cleanse had turned me into a veritable shitting machine. I was so regular, you could set your watch to my bowel movements.

While I had never gotten the rubber-rope results that Tim did, by the time I returned to grad school, most of the promised benefits of the cleanse had taken hold. My skin glowed, my eyes sparkled, and my hair looked like it belonged in a Breck commercial. I had more energy, and my longtime companions—stomach problems and sinus congestion—were nowhere to be found. And, most importantly, for the first time in my life, I felt like I had taken charge of my own well-being.

During my second week of spring semester classes, an old and often-crotchety film production professor noticed the gallon jug of water I'd taken to carrying around everywhere I went, and stopped class to address me.

"So, Sekoff . . . you sick or something?" he asked.

All eyes turned to face me. Many of my classmates had obviously wondered the same thing. I'd seen them watching me as I took a gulp of water, shaking their heads incredulously while guzzling coffee and soda, or puffing on a cigarette.

"No, sir. I'm not sick."

"Then why are you always carting around that jug?"

"So I won't *get* sick."

"Oh . . ."

He started to say something else, hesitated, then turned away. It was a reaction I would become more and more familiar with in the ensuing years as I became increasingly health conscious: slightly baffled, slightly judgmental, slightly worried that I might know something they didn't—but should.

Tim and I did the cleanse together again one more time before consciously uncoupling, each moving into our own one-bedroom apartment (he got the Colema Board in the breakup; I quickly ordered a new one).

He continued to study health and nutrition, eventually abandoning acting and becoming a highly regarded naturopathic doctor, with his own line of supplements and a bestselling book.

I subsequently took a ride on a dietary pendulum, swinging out to the fringes of eating nothing but raw food and making my own vegan sprouted-seed cheese before swinging back—largely motivated by the desire to not scare away a potential future spouse—to a middle ground of "everything in moderation" healthy eating.

And I continued to fast and cleanse at least once a year—with it becoming progressively easier each time I did. I never proselytized or attempted to convert others to the Church of the High Colonic, but, seeing how good I felt, many of my friends asked if they could join. I helped introduce more than a dozen people to the Ways of the Board, often talking them through the "popping of their colonic cherry"—sometimes over the phone, frequently standing on the other side of a bathroom door.

"Think of a flower opening up for a bee," I'd always tell them while I patiently waited for . . . the *whoosh!*

Oprah's Tears

My wife, Tammy, is the nicest person I've ever known. Bar none. And I've met Tom Hanks. I could count the number of times I've seen her be unkind to someone on Oscar Pistorius's toes.

So when she asks me for something, which is rare, I find it very hard to say no. Even if she's asking for someone else. Say her older sister, Debbie.

Not that I have anything against Debbie, although it's true that we got off on the wrong foot. I had just started dating Tam when Debbie came to town for a visit. I met them for drinks, and Deb said something less than laudatory about her sister— nothing egregious, just your run-of-the-mill sibling snark. But it rubbed me the wrong way and I zinged her back sharply. I mean, I'd been seeing her sister for close to eighteen days at that point, while they'd only known each other their whole lives. The nerve of some people, amirite?!

But, over the ensuing decades, we've gotten along just fine. She was the maid of honor at our wedding (although I could've sworn I saw the slightest bit of hesitation during the "If anyone here has any reason why . . ." part of the ceremony), and has been a loving, supportive aunt to our kids. In fact, there is a long list of relatives I like a lot less than her, including any number I share a bloodline with.

The request-by-proxy came as I was packing for a trip to Chicago to meet with Oprah Winfrey's team about moving all of their online content onto the Huffington Post's platform. Tammy was hoping I could bring something special back for Debbie, who absolutely adores Oprah; a signed cap or T-shirt or photograph—anything personalized by the Big O. Now, I'm not really in the habit of asking for favors from people I'm working with (although the last few years have made grabbing a selfie with any remotely famous person you encounter de rigueur; in fact, I think even the extremely rare ones who act put upon would be insulted if you didn't ask). But I half-heartedly promised to "see what I can do."

The flight to Chicago was uneventful, as was my night at the hotel the company had booked me in: Trump International. Of course, if I'd known then what I know now, I would've retroactively shit the bed or, at a minimum, unplugged the minibar so all the high-end chocolate bars got mushy.

The next day, I met with Team Oprah at their sprawling Harpo Studios building. Along with discussing the benefits of HuffPost's approach to community engagement, we also talked about their company's experiments with online video, something I was especially interested in since we were in the early stages of building HuffPost Live, our livestreaming video network.

Toward the end of the meeting, Oprah popped her head into the room. She was wearing sweats and didn't have any makeup on—but even workaday Oprah lit up the room. The effect of seeing someone in the flesh who you've been enraptured by on TV for so many years is, I'd imagine, akin to a devout Christian seeing Jesus stroll into the rectory. Luckily, no stigmata materialized following Oprah's brief appearance.

The plan for that night was to screen a "best of the Oprah Show" episode in front of a studio audience, then do a live show, featuring Oprah, that would simultaneously air on Oprah's OWN cable network and livestream on Oprah.com, utilizing a host of the digital tools we were going to use on HuffPost Live: guests joining the conversation via Skype, real-time comments coming in on Facebook, and interaction with the studio audience.

I took a seat in the last row of the jam-packed audience, just in front of the table from where Oprah's executive producer oversaw the production.

The live show went off like a dream. It featured a teary-eyed conversation between Oprah and Iyanla Vanzant, the charismatic relationship expert who had been a mainstay on Oprah's syndicated show in the late '90s until a misunderstanding led to a falling out that lasted for over a decade.

And the new media elements came together perfectly: as the topics veered from the lifelong trauma of childhood molestation to abortion to alcoholism to mother-daughter communication, Oprah deftly pulled in the people on Skype, picked out Facebook comments that pinballed the discussion in new and surprising directions, and elicited touching contributions from the studio audience.

It was a masterful and moving performance, and everyone in the room was, at some point, crying—including Oprah. Including me; I probably blubbered my way through half a packet of Kleenex.

After the show ended, the audience sat in their seats, simultaneously buzzing with excitement and emotionally drained. We finally started filing out. My path took me past the desk Oprah and Iyanla had been seated at. That's when I noticed them: a pair of crumpled tissues in Oprah's spot. Remembering my wife's request for an Oprah memento, I was seized with the impulse to slip them into my coat pocket. *Who needs a signed T-shirt when I can deliver Oprah's tears!*

But just as I was about to filch them, a bubbly young production assistant scurried up and told me to follow her. I cast a crestfallen look at the tissues as we headed backstage to see Oprah, who, like the audience, was still amped from the show. She wrapped me in a warm embrace. Still no stigmata, but I could feel my forehead flush.

I told her I'd been blown away by how much immediacy and vitality the new media elements had added to the show—and how they'd made the audience, both in the studio and watching at home, such a dynamic part of the conversation.

She nodded; she'd felt it too.

"I know this is going to sound ridiculous," I said, trying not to gush, "especially seeing how you've basically ruled over television for the past twenty years, but, I gotta say, you were born for the Internet, which is all about community and connecting and authenticity and breaking down the wall between a performer and the audience. You belong online . . ."

I could almost hear her doing the mental calculations about how much less it would've cost to start a digital network than the $300 million it had taken to launch OWN.

Another hug, and she was on her way.

Pumped up on proximity and purpose, I called after her: "Oprah, the revolution may not be televised, but it *will* be live-streamed . . . and Facebooked and tweeted!"

She stopped in her tracks and turned back to me: "Say that again."

"The revolution may not be televised, but it *will* be live-streamed . . . and Facebooked and tweeted!"

"I like that." She called over an assistant and had her write down what I'd said.

She patted me on the cheek and sauntered to her dressing room, softly repeating the line.

I was giddy. Not just because Oprah had liked my updated riff on Gil Scott-Heron, but at the promise this new approach to creative conversation held for what we were planning to do with HuffPost Live. I felt a little like Jon Landau had upon seeing Bruce Springsteen in concert in 1974: "I have seen the future of online talk . . ."

Back at the hotel (again, apologies for not pissing in the Trump-branded plant holder), I suddenly remembered that I'd forgot to remember about bringing home some Oprah swag for Debbie. Crap! Maybe I could get someone at Harpo to send me a hat.

I emptied my pockets on the nightstand: wallet, room key, lip balm, the used Kleenex I'd gone through during the show.

I had already tossed the soiled tissues into the trash when my *Eureka!* moment hit. It was a decision as simple as it was shifty: like Jesus turning water into wine, I was going to transform my snot into Oprah's tears.

Although I'd long been a proponent of the value of utilizing a little white lie—and occasionally a big black one—when called for, I preferred not to lie to my wife. At the same time, who would this relatively minor deception hurt? It's not like Oprah's actual tears might heal a sick child (although they might), or have any real worth outside the realm of oddball memorabilia. Plus, it's not like anyone was going to be nutty enough to test the DNA to determine the provenance of the tears, right? (Nervous thought: maybe they would be!)

But there was no denying what a special, one-of-a-kind gift I'd (theoretically) be delivering. And what delight I'd be bringing to Debbie's day. Who was I to rob her of that joy?

So I put the tissues into a plastic bag and brought them home.

When I gave them to Tammy, she was initially confused: "You got my sister secondhand tissues?"

"Not just tissues; tissues laden with the physical manifestation of a TV icon's raw emotions. These are Oprah's tears!"

She was warming to the idea. She rolled the concept around her mind like a fine brandy in a crystal snifter. "Yes, Oprah's tears!" She gave the baggie holding the tissues a closer look. "How come there's no mascara on them?"

"Um . . . I'm not sure," I replied, my mind scrambling for a semiplausible explanation. "Maybe she just dabbed the corner of her eye. Or maybe she uses some top-of-the-line no-run makeup. All I know is I got those tissues off the desk right where she was sitting. And weeping."

This must be how it starts, I thought, picturing Haldeman, Ehrlichman, and Nixon going all-in on the "Rose Mary Stretch" explanation for the infamous eighteen-and-a-half-minute Watergate tape gap.

But Tammy was sold. Debbie would love it! We even had a particularly passionate Oprah Tears–inspired roll in the hay to commemorate my shrewdness in snagging the tissues.

I was now fully committed. And that much closer to burning in hell.

The owner of the trophy shop, a short, balding Armenian with a bristly white mustache, was having a very hard time understanding exactly what I wanted him to do with the tissues I was showing him. And not just because his English was limited. He also had no idea who—or what—an "Oprah" was, even after my halfway decent "You get a car, you get a car . . . everybody gets a car!" impression.

But eventually we worked it out, and a week later Tammy was hand-delivering the result: a Lucite box showcasing a pair of crinkly, mucus-stained tissues mounted on a black base, with a small plaque reading "Oprah's Tears" along with the date they were secreted and gathered.

The gift was a huge hit, earning me waves of gratitude from my wife and her sister, congrats from their parents, and accolades from all who came to Debbie's house and saw it displayed in a place of honor. The circle of deception continues to expand to this day.

If, as they say, the cover-up is worse than the crime, I'm definitely looking at multiple counts of felonious flimflammery. Should this story ever be published, I imagine the best I'll be able to hope for is concurrent sentences.

A month after my Chicago trip, I learned Oprah was doing another livestreaming show, this time from her studio in Los Angeles. Arianna was one of the guests, so I went along to help her prep.

During the live broadcast, Oprah spotted me standing in the wings. I noticed a look of recognition roll across her face. She waited until she knew the camera was on someone else, then looked me in the eye and mouthed the words "The revolution!" But she stretched it out, as if she was enunciating it very precisely, so it became "The rev-oh-loo-shun!!"

It took all of my willpower to not burst out laughing. I gave her an exaggerated thumbs-up.

After the show, we crossed paths backstage and briefly chatted. I gave her an update on HuffPost Live, and she told me that the livestreaming broadcast in Chicago was supposed to be a one-off, but she was so taken with all the things I'd been so enthused about after that episode that she'd decided to do a series of Skype-and-Facebook-powered online shows.

Before we parted, she gave me a hug and whispered in my ear, in the best Oprah impersonation anyone could do, "The rev-oh-loo-shun!"

Okay, so I'd become Revolution Boy. Not a problem. I was on Oprah's radar, and so was HuffPost Live. It was almost enough to make me cry. I checked my pockets for a tissue. You never know when someone else will be in need of a very special gift.

The Snakeman Cometh

All the big tourist attractions in '60s-era Miami had a star performer.

At the Monkey Jungle—"Where humans are caged and monkeys run wild"—it was Bulu, a six-foot, six-hundred-pound gorilla that, according to the brochures, was so strong he could rip a truck tire in half (although all I ever saw him do was roll one across his too-small cage).

At the Parrot Jungle—"The world's most colorful attraction"—it was Pinky, a photogenic cockatoo that pedaled a tiny bicycle along a high wire and rode a miniature rocket ship to a plastic moon.

At the Seaquarium—"This sea showplace is no place like home"—it was Bebe, Suzy, and Squirt, some of the dolphins that played Flipper on TV; every two hours they would jump through hoops, knock down bowling pins, and, for the grand finale, leap twenty feet into the air to snatch a cigarette from a trainer's mouth.

At the Serpentarium—"Look danger in the eye!"—it was a herpetologist named Bill "the Snakeman" Haast, a local legend who, by the mid-1960s, had been bitten by deadly snakes over one hundred times, often coming close to dying. Nevertheless, dozens of times a day, he would entertain his customers by capturing cobras, mambas, rattlesnakes, and a variety of vipers with his bare hands, then "milking" their venom, to be used for scientific research.

I'd been to the first three many times with my family. But, for some reason, we'd never gone to the Serpentarium. That doesn't mean I was thrilled when we were informed that our fifth-grade class would be taking a field trip there. Indeed, I was less than enthusiastic.

I had never been one of those little boys who nursery rhymes described as being made of "frogs and snails and puppy dog tails." Snails were slimy, touching a frog could give you warts (at least according to my mother), and what kind of sick bastard would cut the tail off a puppy, for christsakes? So spending the day in the midst of over five hundred snakes—many of them poisonous—was not on my ten-year-old self's bucket list.

And I wasn't sure how I felt about Bill Haast. He was regularly lauded by local media as a hero; he'd been bitten by deadly snakes so many times his blood could be used as an antivenom, and he frequently flew around the world to help save the lives of snakebite victims. But my friends and I all found him a little creepy. It was probably a serious case of projection, but with his stern gaze, dark eyes, and raspy voice, we felt there was something reptilian about him—as if all that venom coursing through his veins had altered his DNA, making him a roadside Gorgon, part man, part snake. We joked that he probably pronounced his name "Haasssssssssssssss-t."

The bus ride from school to the Serpentarium was utterly fascinating. Not because we were studying up on snakes, but because we were studying the interaction between our two teachers.

The start of the school year had delivered a shock to the entire student body of West Lab Elementary: the arrival of our first unabashedly sexy teacher, Mrs. Meadows. Traditionally, our teachers were either old, fat, matronly, homely, desiccated, grotesque, riddled with moles—or some unappealing combination thereof. As a staff, they possessed the collective sex appeal of a cloister of mummified nuns.

Mrs. Meadows, on the other hand, was young, pretty, tall, blonde, curvaceous, and hip. She wore miniskirts, white vinyl Nancy Sinatra boots, and thick mascara on both her upper and lower lashes. She was Malibu Barbie come to life.

The first time she pulled into the school parking lot in her canary-yellow Corvette Stingray and eased herself out, one go-go booted calf and uncovered thigh following the other, gently straightened the hem of her miniskirt, then sashayed into the building, it was a moment as mind-blowing for the denizens of West Lab as the shift from black-and-white Kansas to Technicolor Oz had been for Dorothy.

And I was among the thirty randomly selected students in her inaugural class (god bless you, luck of the draw!).

The other thirty fifth-graders were being taught by Miss Rolfe, a legendarily strict—and bizarre-looking—woman who'd been at our school forever. She was a combination of Olive Oyl, the Wicked Witch of the West (to keep the Oz analogies going), and Hogwarts's "Mad-Eye" Moody, since her defining physical characteristic was a pair of eyes that were constantly moving around behind Coke-bottle glasses. And when I say "constantly moving," I mean actually spinning around like a couple of blood-shot dervishes. You never could tell what she was looking at; in fact, the only time she looked you square in the eye was when she was talking to a kid on the other side of the room. And she dressed like a bashful Mother Superior. A burka would be her idea of showing a little skin.

The bus ride would've made for a great psych experiment—it was like we were riding in a giant yellow Skinner box. Miss Rolfe and her students were seated on the right; Mrs. Meadows and her class were on the left. Everyone was quiet, but for completely different reasons. Miss Rolfe had hectored her kids into silence ("If I hear another word, we'll turn this bus around!"); they kept their heads down and their eyes averted. Our side was just trying to do Mrs. Meadows a solid; we knew she was desperate to avoid a confrontation with her flinty colleague (it's not that we were so insightful; before the trip, she'd beseeched us to "not upset Miss Rolfe"). She clearly wanted to be the groovy, easygoing, New Generation teacher but was as leery of Rolfe's wrath—and as unsettled by her gyroscope eyeballs—as the rest of us.

So we rode along like a mini divided Germany—the aisle serving as our Berlin Wall—Frau Rolfe and Fräulein Meadows up front exchanging silent glances across the invisible barbed wire.

The hush was replaced by murmuring and more than a few gasps as we pulled into the Serpentarium parking lot and all looked up at the massive thirty-five-foot-high concrete statue of a hooded king cobra that towered over the building. With its black, beady eyes, realistic shimmering paint job, and long forked tongue jutting out menacingly, it looked less like a promotional landmark and more like a temporarily dormant leviathan, waiting for a bolt of lightning or atomic blast to wake it from its slumber and set it on a path of murderous destruction—and an inevitable battle with one of the similarly terrifying creatures that haunted Saturday afternoon TV screens. He was primed to sink his fangs into the neck of Godzilla, Rodan, or Mothra—and if that involved gobbling up a busload of fifth-graders in the process, so be it.

A slight shiver ran from my overactive imagination down my spine, then took a few spins around my asshole, like dirty bathwater circling a drain. *Why had my parents signed the goddamn permission slip?!*

Miss Rolfe led her charges off the bus first, reminding them: "No talking, no horseplay, no wandering away from the group. You are here to learn, *not* to have fun."

As my class rose from our seats—and after checking to make sure Miss Rolfe was out of earshot—Mrs. Meadows softly told us: "You are here to learn *and* to have fun . . ." She flashed us an impish grin, and my thoughts turned from killer cobras to how long I should wait before asking her to marry me.

I, like all the boys in my class—hell, the whole school—and probably more than a few of the girls, had an enormous crush on Mrs. Meadows (who, rumor had it, had recently been divorced). I found the intensity of my feelings so disturbing that I had begun looking for flaws in her appearance that might break the spell. All I had come up with so far were two barely detectable acne scars on her left cheek, just above the jawline. So I remained besotted—although I had no real way of processing my attraction. Like Brigitte Bardot or Jayne Mansfield, everything about her seemed over-the-top, overripe, and unattainable. Plus, I had no clue how sex actually worked—though something told me that once I figured it out, she'd likely break me in two doing it. (Cue the borscht-belt comic: ". . . but what a way to go!")

In the lead-up to the field trip, I had sketched out a half-baked plan: I would stay as close to Mrs. Meadows as possible so that if any of the snakes or other wild animals we encountered freaked her out, I could comfort her. Or, more likely, I'd be the one freaking out—but either way I'd end up nestled against her ample and no-doubt pillowy bosom.

My cockamamie scheme hit a snag soon after we were introduced to Don and Kathy, our Serpentarium tour guides. Don was a strapping guy in his late twenties, with a tangle of dark hair, a thick mustache, and a gap-toothed smile; he almost flattened a couple of my classmates as he briskly took his place next to Mrs. Meadows, leaving Kathy to deal with Miss Rolfe and her class.

"We'll meet you guys at the snake show . . . if the crocs and gators don't get you first," he called out to the other group as he shot Mrs. Meadows a smug, flirty grin and led us through a pair of glass doors. I hated him already.

The first part of the tour involved us walking down a long, dark hallway, peering into a seemingly endless series of illuminated glass cages built into the wall, each containing a different species of snake. The variety of serpents on display was impressive but, in general, snakes—especially snakes in cages—don't do a hell of a lot. Mostly they coil up, sleep, and wait to be fed. Occasionally one would poke up its head and flick out its tongue—but, in terms of entertainment value, not exactly a cockatoo riding a bike across a high wire.

And Don's tour patter was too cute by half, filled with corny jokes like "How do you measure a snake? In inches, 'cause they don't have any feet!" And "Why don't snakes need to weigh themselves? Because they have their own scales!" I noticed that Mrs. Meadows always laughed at his punch lines, but I couldn't tell if she actually found them funny or was just being polite.

Don's blatant attempts to charm Mrs. Meadows were really pissing me off. Why couldn't we have gotten Kathy as our guide, or some guy with less age-appropriate interests? I'd seen plenty of men—bus drivers, school crossing guards, camp counselors—who liked puffing up their egos by flirting with young girls. And our class had a number of cute ones, including the Hastings twins, who were tall for their age and could easily pass for twelve—maybe even thirteen.

My mental detour down Pedophile Lane was cut short by a sudden eruption of gasps and groans. As I rounded a corner, I saw the cause: inside a much bigger glass enclosure lay a massive snake with an enormous lump in the middle of its body. This, according to Don, was a Burmese python that had swallowed a suckling pig whole and was in the process of digesting it. I noticed more than a few knees buckling—including my own. It wasn't just the grotesqueness of the python's weirdly bulging belly; our class had just finished reading *Charlotte's Web*, so the image of poor Wilbur or one of his porcine pals trapped inside this giant snake, slowly being dissolved by powerful digestive juices, felt personal—and unsettling.

Totally misreading the room, Don cheerfully explained the anatomical anomalies that made it possible for a python to open its jaws "wide enough to swallow the average fifth grader," then made another dumb joke about a snake's favorite dessert: "a pie-thon!" I was thrilled to see Mrs. Meadows sneer and take a step away from him. Sensing an opening, I tried to sidle up to her, but there were too many tightly bunched kids between us. At least the shine had dimmed on Don's Marlin-Perkins-meets-Henny-Youngman shtick.

But instead of dialing things back, Don doubled down: "Stay close to me, everyone," he said, lowering his voice. "Our next stop is the crocodile and alligator pit—and it's feeding time!"

This announcement had an immediate and intense physical effect on me, like what happens when Bruce Banner gets mad. But instead of turning from a mild-mannered scientist into the Incredible Hulk, I transformed from a lovesick schoolboy into a quivering mass of dread—the Incredible Anxiety Attack. My heart started racing, my breathing became shallow, my blood ran cold.

Growing up in Miami, kids were presented with wildly divergent messages about alligators. On the one hand, they were regularly depicted as lovable rascals on billboards, postcards, and Saturday morning cartoons like *Wally Gator*, Hanna-Barbera's happy-go-lucky, porkpie-hat-wearing "swingin' alligator of the swamp." At the same time, we were taught from a young age that they were finely honed killing machines, armed with powerful jaws, rows of snaggly teeth, spiky, whiplike tails, and the ability to reach a top land speed of twenty miles per hour for short bursts.

Plus, there was the way they lurked in murky waters, with only their beady eyes above the surface, waiting for their prey to approach before suddenly springing into deadly action. As a kid whose backyard abutted a lake where gators lived, and who'd been repeatedly warned about the dangers of playing too close to the water's edge, their splashing, thrashing, chomping attacks—seen regularly on *Mutual of Omaha's Wild Kingdom*—haunted my dreams.

So I hovered back a little as my classmates gathered around the disconcertingly shallow pit that housed a couple of gators and two massive crocodiles—a twelve-foot, eighteen-hundred-pound Nile croc named Cookie, and a slightly smaller American croc named Sam that had a stump for a tail. According to Don, Sam had mistaken his own tail for a rival coming to steal his food and chomped down hard enough to self-amputate. *Jesus*, I thought, *if that motherfucker is vicious enough—and stupid enough—to bite off part of its own body, what would he do with my tender and delicious ass?*

It didn't help my primordial panic when Don disclosed that Cookie had learned to climb out of the pit and would occasionally stroll around the grounds until someone showed up with a "croc stick"—at which point the giant reptile would crawl back into the enclosure.

What?! This flesh-eating predator that, fun fact, has only two muscles to open its mouth but forty to close it, can climb out of its pit? Then why not make the pit lower or the walls higher? *And what the hell is a "croc stick"—and where can I get one, Don?*

As I made a vow to never turn my back on Cookie the Croc, Don offered up another of his groaners: "What's the difference between alligators and crocodiles? You'll see one later, and the other you'll see in a while!" Not getting the laugh he expected, Don started singing: "See ya' later alligator, in a while crocodile!"

I was about to inform him that if you gotta explain a joke, it's probably not worth telling—but was cut short when Don announced he had "a special treat for us." My hope that this would involve him taking a flying leap into Cookie and Sam's lair was dashed when he reached into a small wooden crate and pulled out two chickens, dead but unplucked.

Whistling to get the reptiles' attention, he tossed the carcasses into the pit. The crocs both leapt up, each catching a chicken in their gaping maw before it hit the ground. Chomp, chomp . . . and the birds were gone.

Except for two boys, Richard and Larry—one who liked eating paste, and one who'd bragged about putting firecrackers in a frog's mouth on the Fourth of July, then watching it explode—the class appeared unnerved by this display, as did Mrs. Meadows. We were no strangers to the verities of the food chain, but between the baby pig in the python and these chickens, we'd already seen half a barnyard polished off—and it wasn't even noon. What fresh acts of animal kingdom barbarism awaited?

Right on cue, we were joined by Miss Rolfe's class and led to the staging area for the tour's big climax: Bill Haast extracting the venom from a series of deadly snakes.

While we took our seats on the grass, Haast and his wife Clarita, an exotic-looking woman with arched brows and heavily made-up eyes, took their positions, both wearing crisp, white lab coats. I noticed a sign: "There is nothing more exciting than watching danger from a safe distance." But I soon realized Haast's definition of "a safe distance" was way more liberal than mine: he was going to be handling these poisonous vipers just a few feet from where we sat.

Clarita, holding a microphone close to her mouth and narrating the action in a calm, even tone, let the drama of what we were watching speak for itself as time and again her husband, employing a curved metal stick, would pull a poisonous snake out of a box and then, using one hand to "charm" it, grab the back of its head with other. He would then force the snake's fangs into the plastic top of a test tube and watch as the venom dripped down. This feat never failed to elicit a combination of gasps, shrieks, and gleeful applause.

As Haast repeated this death-defying routine with a variety of lethal species—diamondback rattler, green mamba, Malayan pit viper, European asp—Clarita told us that her husband had gotten his first poisonous snake bite at age twelve, landing him in the hospital for a week; that he built up his immunity by injecting himself daily with a mix of venoms from more than a dozen kinds of snakes; and that the venom they collected was being used to treat people suffering from multiple sclerosis and arthritis.

She also shared a delightful story about the time a cotton-mouth had bitten his hand, causing his finger to turn black almost immediately. Concerned that the venom would spread, he had Clarita snip off the end of his finger with garden shears. I wasn't sure whom I admired more, him for asking or her for doing it. (Romantic kid that I was, I couldn't help but wonder, *Will I ever fin• someone who loves me enough to lop off an extremity?* I was pretty sure that Mrs. Meadows would.)

Soon it was time for the grand finale: Haast was going to "milk" a king cobra, which, Clarita informed us, was "the longest venomous snake in the world . . . its venom can kill an elephant in just a few hours."

Given this, I was more than a little surprised when Haast's assistants placed a glass-fronted cage on the ground a few feet from us. Surely this elephant killer called for just a wee bit of extra precaution, no? Apparently not. I began plotting potential escape routes.

Haast unlatched a door on the side of the cage and stepped back. A moment later, an enormous snake slithered out—"a six-teen footer," Clarita reported—and he didn't seem pleased to be there. We all instinctively scooted back as Haast controlled the agitated viper using his curved stick. Suddenly, the cobra reared up, with at least a third of its body standing erect, showing its fangs and hissing loudly. Holy shit—the thing was practically eye to eye with Haast, who held up his right hand, trying to draw the snake's attention. The viper flared its hood and made a few lunges as it advanced across the floor. Haast held his ground, waiting for the right moment to make his patented snatch-the-back-of-the-head move.

Everyone in the crowd was holding their breath. All at once, Haast reached for the snake, which turned its head and struck, catching him on the forearm. The snake handler, who hadn't said a word the whole time, released a barely audible "Ouch." Steeling himself, he grabbed the snake with his other hand, swiftly carried it to the waiting vial, and drained the rest of its venom. He then gave Clarita a look. You could see the concern in her eyes but she was a pro and, without changing her tone, calmly declared, "And that concludes the show for today . . ."

Haast's assistants speedily got the king cobra back into its box while he hurried toward his office, clutching his arm.

Visibly shaken, Don, Kathy, and our teachers scrambled to get us to our feet and led us off to look at George, the attraction's giant Aldabra tortoise. Everyone was on edge, worried about what was going to happen to Haast. We began debating the possible outcomes.

"She said that he had built up his immunity by taking venom every day, so that should save him . . ."

"But she also said that a king cobra could kill an elephant; just imagine what it'll do to a man."

"But he's been bitten like a bajillion times before . . ."

"Can you believe he barely said a thing? I guarantee you: if a king cobra bit me, I'd say a lot more than 'Ouch!'"

As the back-and-forth continued, I tried to ascertain what was happening with Haast but couldn't see anything. So I told Mrs. Meadows that I had to use the restroom, which I knew was near the front office.

But she wouldn't let me go alone and asked the class who else needed to use the bathroom. Unfortunately for me, Adam Pliskin's bladder was full. Adam was a notorious stick-in-the-mud, the kind of kid who complains if a substitute teacher wants to show a movie, and who'd love to earn a few brownie points by narcing me out.

I didn't really have to pee, so I slipped into the stall and flushed the toilet to cover for the lack of a stream. Adam was still standing at the urinal when I came out. I thought about softening him up by complimenting the Cub Scout uniform he had on, but one look at that stupid yellow neckerchief spread across his shoulders told me I'd never pull it off. Even the word "neckerchief" filled me with contempt. So I decided to try the direct approach: "You want to go see what's happening with Haast?"

"Nah."

"Aren't you curious?"

"Nah."

What a dickhead. I next tried a little psychological jujitsu. "Doesn't the Cub Scout Oath say you should help other people at all times?"

It didn't work. "That doesn't include breaking the rules, buttwipe."

So I threatened to kick his ass if he told on me. I was a scrawny, small-for-my-age ten-year-old, and far from a tough kid. But Adam was even smaller. He was one of the few people in my class I was pretty confident I could take; and the rest of them were girls.

So, with Adam's "you and what army?" trailing behind me, I left the bathroom and made my way toward where I thought Haast was. The place was abuzz with activity. I noticed Clarita talking on the phone; she looked composed but very focused. But I couldn't see her husband. So I moved a little closer and spotted him slumped in a chair, his left arm lying limply in his lap. I couldn't tell if he was feeling the effects of the bite or merely bored. Can one ever feel blasé about having deadly neurotoxins mainlined into your central nervous system, even if it has happened over one hundred times before?

After a moment, Haast turned his head toward me and we locked eyes. Feeling like a Peeping Tom caught in a cop's flashlight, I froze, then gave him a sheepish wave. He didn't react at first. Then he stuck his tongue out at me. In my memory, it was thin, forked, and vibrating. Seeing my reaction, he smiled, then looked away.

I gradually became aware of sirens approaching. Glancing at the entryway, I saw an ambulance arrive. Two paramedics jumped out and pulled a gurney out of the back of the vehicle.

Suddenly, I felt something on my shoulder. Thinking it might be a runaway snake, Cookie the Croc, or Adam Pliskin come to call my bluff, I twisted around violently—and saw that it was Mrs. Meadows.

"Are you okay?" she asked.

She didn't seem mad at me for wandering off but I just stared at her, speechless. "Were you worried about Mr. Haast?"

I nodded my head. And then it happened. She pulled me to her, hugging my head against her chest, which was even more pillowy than I had imagined. I savored the smell of her lilac perfume, intoxicated by the scent—and her touch. Opening my left eye—the one not nestled in her cleavage—I thought I could see Don the tour guide watching us in the distance. Suck it, Donny Boy. *What •i• the victorious fifth gra•er say to the loser tour guide? Sorry, pal, but you're hiss-tory!*

Mrs. Meadows patted my cheek, called me a "sweet boy," then took my hand and led me back to where our class was standing. The rest of the boys—especially Adam Pliskin—gave me the evil eye. I was pretty sure that Miss Rolfe did too, but with her you could never be sure.

A coda:

In 1977, a six-year-old boy who was trying to get Cookie the Croc's attention by tossing sea grapes at it, slipped and fell into the croc pit. In the blink of an eye, the crocodile lunged and clamped the boy in its powerful jaws. Rescuers jumped into the pit and eventually got the beast to loosen its grip by poking it in the eye with a stick. But it was too late; the boy died en route to the hospital.

The next day, Bill Haast pumped nine shots from a Luger pistol into Cookie. Then, because it was too heavy to move, he buried the dead reptile in the same place where the boy was killed.

Seven years later, Haast closed the Serpentarium. Even after doing so, he continued to work with snakes—and inject himself with their venom—until he died at the age of one hundred. By the time of his death, he'd been bitten by poisonous snakes close to two hundred times and was credited with saving over twenty people who would have died without receiving a pint of his antibody-rich blood.

The giant concrete king cobra that loomed over the building was donated to a local high school but crumbled while it was being transported.

Mrs. Meadows and I didn't end up getting married, which is just as well. Now that I know what goes where, she definitely would've broken me in two. But what a way to go . . .

"The McDonald's of Sex"

Her name was Holly. She had wavy auburn hair, green eyes, and freckles on her nose. She laughed at my jokes, thought I was "cute," and was willing to do whatever it would take to make me smile. As I saw it, the only thing standing in the way of our happily-ever-after was the cum-stained sheet of plexiglass between us, and the fact that it would cost me five •ollars to keep talking to her for another three minutes.

Two weeks after graduating from high school, I turned eighteen. To celebrate these back-to-back milestones, my parents agreed to fund a solo trip to New York City, provided I found a suitable (i.e., no-cost) place to stay.

Luckily, my friend Steve had moved to New York earlier that year and graciously said I could crash at his apartment. I didn't realize until I got there that it was a tiny one-room studio with only a queen-sized bed that we'd be sharing—or that Steve slept in the nude. But free was free, and Steve had already accepted that I wasn't interested in "exploring my bi side"—though I will admit to wearing gym shorts to bed instead of my usual Fruit of the Loom undies.

As the 1976–77 president of the Coral Gables Senior High drama club, I felt honor-bound to make a Broadway show the first stop on my New York adventure. I opted for Lily Tomlin's award-winning *Appearing Nitely*, and was lucky to score a last-minute ticket in the sixth row. She deserved every clap of her extended standing ovation.

Having checked the culture box, I set my sights on decidedly less high-minded fare: a visit to Times Square, which, at the time, was the Valhalla of Sleaze. As a longtime fan of the pornographic arts, this was like a Catholic going to the Vatican—though I doubt the pope had giant neon signs boasting: "Live Nude Girls!"

New York in the summer of '77 was far from the urban version of the Happiest Place on Earth it has become today. This was a city on the verge of financial collapse, a place of roiling racial tensions and dread over the Son of Sam killings. Indeed, just a couple of weeks before my trip, the *New York Daily News* had published a chilling letter from the killer in which he offered his take on the troubled metropolis: "Hello from the gutters of N.Y.C. which are filled with dog manure, vomit, stale wine, urine and blood." Just the place for a sheltered, neurotic kid from the couldn't-be-less-mean streets of Coral Gables.

It says something about the lure of the lewd, the powerful pull of the prurient, that none of these troubles were on my mind as the cab dropped me off on Forty-Second Street. Even in the middle of the day, a thick layer of seaminess hung in the air, a sordid cloud rivaling the toxic smog choking Beijing.

I took in the scene: grimy establishments with names like the PlayPen, Adulterama, Peep-O-Rama, Follies Burlesk, and House of Paradise; and garish neon signs promising "25 cent

Mini-Movies," "Sex Toys," and "Live Acts on Stage: 'Seeing is Believing!'" One X-rated shop had a sign over its door that said:
"Top Floor
Sensitive Meeting Place
6 Lovely Girls"
I could just picture the six scantily clad women empathetically listening to a group of soft-spoken men sitting on beanbag chairs talk about always being picked last in gym class or making the case for why men *can*, in fact, have women friends they aren't trying to sleep with.

But none of these businesses drew more than a passing interest from me. My porn pilgrimage was pointing me toward a single destination, the perv's holiest of holies: Show World Center, a four-story, twenty-two-thousand-square-foot monument to the economic power of lechery. Promoted as "The McDonald's of Sex," the kinky superstore had something for everyone: dirty books, stag films, peep shows, and live sex acts.

As I made way inside, I could feel my pulse quicken and my chest tighten with a familiar mix of anticipation and angst—apparently you can take the boy out of his father's porn-containing closet, but you can't take the closet out of the boy.

I decided to ease into things by perusing the store's extensive selection of sexual "novelties"; it ran the gamut from A (anal beads) to W (whips and waterproof vibrators)—it seems X, Y, and Z are sorely underserved by the sex-toy industry.

Beginning to feel acclimated, I was ready to check out the private booths where, for a quarter a minute, you could access an array of Super 8 skin flicks. I got change from an unsmiling, long-haired guy who patrolled the booth area wearing one of those metal change dispensers around his waist like the concession guys at the ballpark. *Get your filth here, ice-cole filth! Blow jobs, cum shots, double penetration!*

It took me a couple of tries before I found a booth that felt clean enough to enter (prerequisite #1: no wadded-up tissues on the floor). As I closed the door behind me, my lungs burned with the acrid odor of disinfectant. But at least it was sanitized!

I watched a couple of hard-core shorts but was quickly bored—this was exactly the kind of stuff I'd been seeing at home for the last six years. So I decided to up the ante and give the "Live Sex Show" a try; that was certainly something I couldn't find hidden in my dad's closet.

I was unable to locate the scowling change guy, so I walked over to the cashier to find out how the sex show thing worked. He was a short, muscular Puerto Rican with a collection of chains around his neck, holding, among other things, a gold cross, a St. Christopher medal, and a small red, white, and blue Puerto Rican flag.

He explained that I'd go into a booth like the one for the Super 8s, but that when I put a dollar into a payment slot, a panel would lift and I'd see some form of live sex show. "Could be a guy and a chick," he explained helpfully, "could be two chicks; could be a chick playing with herself. And sometimes there is a woman who does things like smoke a cigarette with her snatch, or shoot a hard-boiled egg out of her *chocha*—but not today; she called in sick."

He seemed like a fount of knowledge, so I asked him his name—it was Carlos—and a few more questions about the live show. He laughed and said, "You curious, huh?" I admitted that I was intrigued by this foreign and forbidden world. He jokingly suggested I should apply for a job. I told him I had worked at a bookstore, but that we sold *text*books not *sex*books.

"Oh, no, you'd have to start off on mop patrol," Carlos said, turning serious. "We call them spew swabbers. Or cum cleaners. Or jizz scrubbers."

"What . . . and give up show business?!" I said, tossing out the classic circus-joke punch line. But he didn't get it. So I got some dollar bills and headed to the live sex show booths. The only one that was unoccupied was at the far end of a semicircle of doors.

With a tingle of excitement at trying something new, I slid a dollar into the slot. After a moment, a thin wood panel pulled up, revealing a small window. It made me think of a prisoner getting his meal delivered through a slot in his cell door.

It took a second for my eyes to adjust and settle on the scene in front of me: a naked woman lying on a cushioned massage table with an equally naked man standing between her legs, rhythmically thrusting his hips. Yep, they seemed to actually be doing it—though, from my angle, it was hard to tell for sure. He soon picked up the pace, with her offering some standard-issue porn film moans and a half-hearted, "Oh, yeah, baby, fuck me!" Just as they started to change positions—it looked like they were going to go for a modified standing doggie-style—the wood panel slid back into place.

I questioned whether I should put in another dollar. Watching real people have sex in front of me was, in theory, a stimulating concept. But something about it had fallen flat. Watching dirty movies, you got up-close-and-very-personal (sometimes too much so). In comparison, these people seemed a bit distant and detached. It's like how watching sports on TV is so much better than going to a game—why wouldn't you want the best seat in the house? And how about that instant replay?

I put another bill in the payment slot anyway. In for a dime, in for the pop shot, I always say.

When the panel retracted again, I saw that the guy, in fact, was now, in the porn vernacular, "giving it to her from behind." They had both worked up a sweat but seemed no closer to finishing than before. Her eyes were closed as she grasped the table and offered up a few more perfunctory groans. I wondered if she was secretly making a mental grocery list or thinking of what errands she needed to do.

I suddenly became aware that, from my vantage point in the last booth in the semicircle, I was able to see the faces of the other men ogling the sex show. Some looked aroused, some were stone-faced, some had their eyes closed—seeming to have other things on their minds (or in their hands). Voyeurism had never struck me as a team sport, and seeing my fellow oglers kinda creeped me out. It also instantly made me think less of myself. So even before the partition closed, I walked out of the booth, casting one last look at the naked woman, her eyes still squeezed shut, her expression seeming to say: *Note to self: remember to pick up extra K-Y.*

I did a quick check of my erotic encounter scorecard. So far I was 0-for-2. But like a gambler convinced that a winning hand is just one deal away, I decided to head upstairs and give the touted "Live Nude Girls" peep show a try.

Finding an unoccupied, recently decontaminated booth, I thought of Carlos's slogan for the store's cleanup brigade—"You pop it, we mop it!"—and, smiling, stepped inside. The first thing I noticed was that the retractable wood panel was much larger than in the sex show cubicle; more like a full-length mirror than an airplane porthole. Next, I saw that there was a tall stool situated in front of the panel. This gave me pause (ass-germ alert!), but it too looked as if it had been recently doused with disinfectant. Lastly, I noted that the fee-per-viewing was five dollars—the premium one paid for a personalized experience, I concluded. Seemed reasonable.

So I slid a fiver into the slot and took a seat on the stool.

The tall, thin panel slid to the side, revealing a sheet of plexiglass. On the other side of the transparent plastic was a pretty girl with wavy auburn hair, green eyes, and freckles on her nose, sitting on a stool identical to the one I was perched on. She was wearing a chiffony red nightie and matching sheer panties. She didn't look to be much older than me.

"Hey, baby, I'm Holly," she said. "What're you looking for?" She started to undo the nightie.

"Uh, you can keep that on," I said, maybe a little too forcefully. "I kinda just want to talk to you . . ."

"Oh, a talker," she replied, leaving the top of the nightie untied. "What are you, some kind of anthropologist?"

I was momentarily taken aback by her choice of words (today, my inner monologue would probably be telling myself *Check your privilege, asshole,* but this was a more innocent time—at least as far as talking to peep-show girls was concerned).

"Yes and no," I told her. "I think I want to be a writer or an actor. So I'm interested in people, what makes them tick, how they are affected by their circumstances . . ."

"And you prefer to do your research in sex shops?"

I felt my face flush a little. "Well, I'm interested in that side of things too . . ."

"How old are you?"

This also caught me off guard. "Oh, you can see me? I wasn't sure."

"I mean, it's not super clear but, yeah, I can see you," she said.

I unconsciously sat up a little straighter and asked: "So what do most guys want you to do?"

"Get naked, talk dirty, play with myself, press my tits or ass against the glass," she said matter-of-factly. "One guy who comes in a lot likes me to smoke and spread my legs. Another regular asks me to call him nasty names in a British accent. So I guess I'm kind of an actress too." She slipped into an exaggerated *Masterpiece Theatre* inflection for this last bit, then let out a girlish giggle.

I was starting to like her.

"And do most of the men jerk—" I stopped myself. "Uh, pleasure themselves while they're in here?"

"Pretty much. Some guys just want to stare; it's like they're trying to memorize my body. And every now and then I get a talker like you—but they're not usually as cute . . ."

As if on cue, the wood partition slid shut. I wondered if she had a timer on her side and had mastered the art of saying something just before the panel closed that would ensure another five-dollar bill would be inserted.

In any case, it worked. The plexiglass was once more uncovered. I'm fairly sure I detected a satisfied smile on her face.

"Hel-lo again," she said.

"I'm eighteen," I blurted out. "You asked before . . . It was my birthday last week."

"Oh, so you're legal now, are you?"

"I guess so . . ."

She unleashed another giggly laugh.

I felt my face flushing again. Regrouping, I leaned forward on the stool. "So, I know this is probably none of my business . . . and you can tell me to screw off, if it seems too personal . . . but I'm really curious—"

She cut me off: "How'd a nice girl like me end up in a shithole like this?" She didn't seem mad or offended, but I felt foolish.

"When you put it like that," I said, "it sounds really stupid."

"Only a little . . ."

"Time to call the cliché police . . ."

She laughed again. "You're pretty funny," she said. "I can see you becoming a writer."

"Not if I don't seriously up my originality game."

She leaned back on her stool and exhaled.

"It's actually not a very original story, I'm afraid. When I was sixteen, my stepfather started getting a little too cozy with me, so I dropped out of school and ran away from home. Came to New York, struggled, ended up doing some stripping. Had a baby. Struggled some more. A friend who works here told me I could make good money doing this. And I do. I don't love it; it can be really depressing. But, hey, it could be a lot worse."

The panel slid shut. I felt bad that I'd asked her to rehash that, and didn't want to leave things on that note. So I pulled my last five out of my pocket. But, before I could insert it into the slot, it slipped out of my hand and fluttered to the floor. *No!* Under normal circumstances, leaving five dollars on the ground would be a small price to pay to avoid having to touch something that had come into contact with a peep-show booth floor. My mind reeled at the thought of how much jizz those vinyl tiles had seen over the years. But bizarre times sometimes call for revolting measures, so I gingerly picked up the money and put it in the machine.

The panel slid open. I noticed she had retied the bow at the neck of her nightie.

"I thought maybe I had scared you away," she said.

I wanted to reassure her: "No, not at all . . . I just dropped my money."

Her laugh this time was throatier.

"I'm sorry that I made you dredge up all that shit," I said.

"You didn't *make me* do anything . . . I like talking to you."

I didn't know what to say. I felt the sudden impulse to ask her out for dinner. Not to try to sleep with her, but just to keep talking. Would that be ridiculous? Dangerous?

She interrupted my musings. "What about you? I know you said you want to be a writer and all, but you don't exactly strike me as the peep-show type . . ."

"I don't know," I replied. "Just curious, I guess. I'm basically a nice guy—but I've always found the slightly pervy parts of our psyches very compelling. I wrote myself a note the other day. I was thinking about where I see myself heading in the future, y'know, as a person . . . And I wrote: 'I want to be a good man while still being a bad boy.'"

Another laugh. "I like that . . ."

There was an awkward silence. I thought again about asking her out. Maybe just for coffee.

"C'mon, bad boy," she said, "I can't let you have put all that money in and not at least get a little thrill."

She started to undo the nightie again.

"No, really," I protested. "You don't have to do that . . ."

"I know," she said, then pulled the garment over her head. "I want to."

She did a little shimmy, wiggling her pert, perky breasts. "I know they're not very big, but more than a mouthful is a waste, right?"

I made it a point to keep looking her in the eyes. I didn't know who I was more uncomfortable for, me or her. At the same time, I didn't want to be rude.

"Absolutely," I replied. "You're very attractive . . . and sexy. And sweet."

This time, I'm pretty sure it was her who blushed.

And the partition slid back into place.

I sat there for a moment, unsure what I should do. I was out of fives. Should I go back to the cashier and break my last twenty? Would Holly even be there when I returned? Or would it be best to just leave things like this?

I stepped out of the booth and made my way downstairs. Carlos was behind the counter.

"Ya like what you seen?"

"Yeah, yeah. It was great."

I turned and headed for the door.

"Okay, amigo. Come back when you're ready for mop duty."

I waved and walked out of the store.

After letting my eyes adjust to the afternoon light, I glanced up at the sign advertising the "Top Floor Sensitive Meeting Place," and wished like hell that it was more than code for "come get a hand job." I really could've used a welcoming beanbag chair.

I started to hail a cab, but decided I'd rather walk the forty blocks to Steve's apartment.

Snoop's Weed and Khloé Kardashian's Vagina: Doing the Celebrity Tango

For over eleven years, my business card said *Founding Editor, Huffington Post*. If there was a truth-in-advertising law for job titles, it should probably have read *Firefighter*, because that is what I spent a great deal of my time doing: rushing from crisis to crisis, putting out journalistic fires.

This was especially true when we launched HuffPost Live, and the element of live programming was added to the mix. To belabor the metaphor, this was like dousing our office with gasoline and inviting a steady stream of arsonists to swing by for a visit.

Things grew even more combustible once celebrity interviews became a big part of our daily schedule.

In the beginning, our plan was to sprinkle in celebs only now and then, preferring to focus on more serious (and underreported) issues—think multipart series on poverty, campus rape, civil forfeiture, and the destructive role of big money in our politics. Yes, that's right, we were delusional.

But the immutable laws of the Internet soon took hold—including the one that says the vast majority of people are more likely to click on a video to watch a C-list celebrity, say Fran Drescher, weigh in on the nuances of health-care legislation than a Nobel-winning economist. Don't blame me; blame yourselves, America!

So famous faces began appearing in our studios more and more often. And, as a result, I was engulfed in the flames of calamities—real and imagined—so frequently I was starting to look like Jim Carrey's Fire Marshall Bill (*don't worry, folks . . . we're just doing a show!*).

The vast majority of these conflagrations were sparked by a group of people that are commonly found in the orbit of celebrities: the personal publicist, aka the PR rep. Publicists congregate around VIPs the way pilot fish cluster around sharks. And their symbiotic relationship has the same dynamic: like pilot fish, PR people live off the scraps their famous clients leave behind. In exchange, they try to keep the star free from parasites while guiding them through troubled waters.

It's a largely thankless job but, as I found out in short order, most PR people take their role as celebrity guardians far too seriously. When it comes to zealotry, they make ISIS suicide bombers look like rank amateurs.

It's like when you have children: you quickly figure out which of their preschool chums have parents who exhibit the traditional level of protectiveness, and which have a mom or dad who takes the term "helicopter parenting" literally—hovering overhead like a HueyCobra in Nam, ready to rain hellfire and damnation down on any kid foolish enough to touch their precious little one's Goldfish crackers.

These overprotective publicists often treat their clients like a woman I knew (and I'm not saying if she was related to me or not, so don't press me) who partially chewed her daughters' food for them until the oldest finally said, "Mom, please stop; my boyfriend thinks that's really gross!"

The thing is, most people in the news don't need protecting. They are pros who know how to artfully deflect a question they don't want to answer. But bloody battles over what topics a celebrity would and wouldn't discuss were a daily occurrence at HuffPost Live, as were vehement post-interview calls demanding that we change a headline, take down a video, or pretend that a celebrity didn't say the moronic thing they'd just said live on the air.

My first time doing the Publicist Tango came a few months after we'd launched, when one of Khloé Kardashian's three PR people threatened to pull her client from our lineup moments before she was supposed to go live.

A little backstory: While developing HuffPost Live, I had vowed that we would never have on a Kardashian—a clan of glorified grifters I hold responsible for a good portion of the moral, spiritual, and cultural rot that's eating away at American society like a flesh-eating bacteria. And especially not a second-tier sibling like Khloé.

But I am a realist—and a click-whore—so, after numerous entreaties from our editors that "anything Kardashian goes through the roof," I put aside my admittedly elastic core principles and we booked Khloé. We even heavily promoted her upcoming live segment on the HuffPost and AOL front pages, and all over social media. Hey, if you're going to be a ho, you might as well be a successful one (as Kris Jenner probably said at some point).

That's why I was more than a little dismayed when, just a couple of minutes before Khloé's segment was scheduled to start, an associate producer rushed into my office to tell me there was big trouble brewing outside the green room and that I needed to come quick.

I rushed over to find our executive producer, a tall, fiery, Ukrainian woman named Larissa, standing nose to nose with a short, dark-haired woman I soon learned was Khloé's personal publicist. (Khloé, it turns out, had three PR people with her: this woman, another who worked for E!, and a third who repped Kotex, for whom Kardashian was a "brand ambassador." That's right, it took three different women to properly "handle" a D-list reality TV "star." See "cultural rot" above.)

Their back-and-forth had clearly gotten intense. For a minute, I thought Larissa, who was a good foot taller than the other woman, was going to pick the publicist up by the collar and toss her across the room.

I rapidly got to the heart of the beef: the publicist was threatening to block Khloé's appearance unless we promised that our host wouldn't ask a single question about her sister Kim and Kanye West, who had recently announced they were expecting their first child.

Khloé was promoting her work with U by Kotex, an initiative to help educate young girls about their bodies, and that was all the publicist wanted us to cover. I calmly explained that while we were planning to make that the focus of the interview—which was scheduled to last thirty minutes—we also wanted to ask Khloé about other things of interest to our viewers, including her famous family. I reminded the woman that this was Publicity 101: we talk about the thing you want to promote, and we get to ask you about the things we're interested in. And I assured her that we weren't looking to play "gotcha" or make her client look bad—but rather that *we'd* be the ones to look like fools and hacks if we didn't at least ask about the headline-making pregnancy.

She wasn't buying it, even after I made the case that we wouldn't exactly be prying into the private lives of publicity-shy people. After all, Kanye had announced the news onstage at an Atlantic City concert, saying, "Stop the music and make some noise for my baby mama!"; and Khloé had already tweeted about it. I was pretty confident she could handle a softball like, "So how does it feel knowing you're going to be an aunt?"

But the publicist refused to budge. She gave me an ultimatum: no promise re Kim/Kanye, no interview. "We'll walk," she said, crossing her arms across her chest defiantly. We were less than sixty seconds from the scheduled start of the live interview.

Now, under normal circumstances, I would have gladly pointed her toward the door. But we'd been promoting the segment all morning, and I knew it would look bad if we suddenly were Khloé-less. So I tried a different tack:

"Okay, here's the deal," I said, trying to be simultaneously reasonable and menacing. "If your client isn't on the set in the next thirty seconds, I am going to go on the air and spend the next thirty minutes explaining to our viewers why she refused to come on. And then we'll cut short clips of my explanation and keep it on the front page of HuffPost all day."

She chuckled and shrugged, digging in her heels.

"If you think I'm joking, you don't know me very well," I said, glancing at my watch. "You've got twenty seconds . . ." I turned to our stage manager. "Get me a microphone."

As I pivoted to head toward our set, the publicist blinked. "I'll get Khloé," she rasped, clearly choking on the words.

I wish I could tell you that I didn't feel a rush of smug satisfaction, but I'm not that evolved as a person. It took all my self-control not to do a hip-thrusting Ace Ventura victory dance. *Yes!*

And here's the thing: the segment went off without a hitch. Khloé was warm and funny and open, taking Skype calls from our viewers and answering questions about everything from her relationship with Lamar Odom to her struggles with her weight to working with Simon Cowell to Kim and Kanye.

And her vagina. That's right, her vagina.

Sparked by a question from one of our viewers concerned about feminine hygiene, Khloé said, "Are vaginas supposed to smell? 'Cause mine smells like roses."

She also offered the following below-the-waist insights:

"I think vaginas can get you a lot of places in life."

"Vaginas rule the world."

"At the end of the day, a good puss can control any man."

She also weighed in on having sex while menstruating: "I'm not going to bone someone on my period. I don't like people who run red lights. No thanks!"

And that, my friends, is modern celebrity culture in a nutshell: don't you dare ask someone about their spotlight-adoring sister, but they'll be more than happy to prattle on about their vagina for as long as you like.

PS: It should go without saying that the HuffPost story headlined "Khloé Kardashian: My Vagina 'Smells Like Roses'" went through the roof.

Another three-alarm pseudo-catastrophe during our first year came courtesy of Snoop Dogg—who, being Snoop, decided to fire up a blunt toward the end of his live interview. My phone started ringing before the smoke was even out of his lungs.

The first overwrought call came not from a PR person but from one of our sales reps, the guy who handled the account of our main sponsor, Cadillac. Sales Guy was apoplectic at the prospect of having Cadillac associated with . . . gasp! . . . marijuana. He was convinced we were in danger of losing the car company's $3 million ad buy if we didn't "do some serious damage control."

I asked what he had in mind. It's not like we could roll the tape backward and have Snoop un-inhale the weed.

Sales Guy wasn't sure, but among his suggestions: remove the interview from our archives, don't promote it anywhere on our site, issue a statement distancing ourselves from "the actions" (harder to do since our host had also taken a hit of the joint), and a personal call from me to the head of Cadillac.

When I expressed surprise at how quickly Cadillac had reacted, Sales Guy admitted that he actually hadn't heard from the company (*yet*, he added pointedly)—and that his panic was "preemptive but warranted" because he "understands how these things work."

I told him I would wait until someone actually complained before scrambling the jets and going to DEFCON 1. In the meantime, we posted the clip of Snoop with the headline: "Snoop Smokes Weed on HuffPost Live." It started to go viral.

The next call was from our office's designated floor captain, who wanted to remind me that our studio was a no-smoking area, and that our employee handbook guaranteed my staff "the right to a safe and hazard-free workplace." I assured him that Snoop lighting up was definitely an aberration and that we'd be sure not to make guests getting high on air a recurring facet of our programming.

Then I heard from Human Resources. They wanted to let me know that our host's single inhale likely violated a long list of company rules and regulations ("He's got to understand that you can't get stoned at work . . . especially on video!") and that some form of retribution was called for.

I asked what they had in mind. They weren't sure but "everything needs to be on the table."

And so it went for the next few days. Even though we still hadn't heard anything negative from Cadillac—or from anyone else outside our own company—like a snake swallowing its own tail, the pressure to "do something" continued to mount.

Sales Guy insisted that no Cadillac ads run before the Snoop clip, which kept getting picked up by more and more media outlets, and racking up more and more video views.

Designated Floor Captain made us hold a "Building Safety" review session with the entire HuffPost Live staff.

And Human Resources kept pushing me to punish our host. I repeatedly had to talk them into putting down their pitchforks and torches. Slowly, firing gave way to suspension, which gave way to a formal written warning that a next offense would lead to "expeditious dismissal," which gave way to a note he had to sign promising not to "take similar illegal actions on air again."

By the end of the week I was exhausted, having dodged more bullets than Keanu in *The Matrix*.

Luckily, a small respite was in sight: a big presentation and party being held for seven hundred of AOL's top advertisers. I was riding to the event with Mike, the guy who was in charge of all the visuals—photos, videos, sizzle reels—that would be shown that night, when he got a call. From the sound of it, and the looks he was giving me, the person on the other end was asking to get a video clip of Snoop lighting up.

What the fuck? I thought I had put that nonsense to rest.

"Who wants the Snoop clip?" I asked incredulously. "HR? Corporate Security? The producers of *Reefer Madness?*"

"Nope," Mike said. It was Tim Armstrong, our company's CEO, who thought it would be "fun" to start the whole presentation off by showing Snoop and his spliff. "He wants to send the advertisers a message about how cool and edgy we are."

So, after all that . . . *that!* I needed a drink. Or a toke. If only I had Snoop's number.

My Psychic Friends

When it comes to believing, I've never been an easy lay. Among the things I don't believe in:

God.

Ghosts.

Reincarnation.

UFOs.

ESP.

Astrology.

The Bermuda Triangle.

The New World Order.

Bigfoot (actually on the fence on this one).

The Lost City of Atlantis.

That Eddie Haskell died in Vietnam.

And Psychics, Clairvoyants, or Mediums.

I guess you'd call me a skeptic. Or a cynic. Or an asshole (but not because I doubt the paranormal, so that's a different story).

When I was a youngster, the flames of my natural-born incredulity were fanned by watching spoon-bending phenom Uri Geller crash and burn on *Johnny Carson*, and Tony Curtis-as-Houdini mount a public crusade against charlatans who claimed they could communicate with his dead mother.

As a result, I always thought of the Amazing Kreskin as merely the Slightly Engrossing Kreskin and never felt compelled to read Jeane Dixon's syndicated column or call Dionne Warwick's Psychic Friends Network.

Despite this history of disbelief, over the course of my life I've had a number of encounters with those claiming the supernatural power to see the past and predict the future, or channel the spirit of one who has "crossed over to the other side." And, being a cockeyed pessimist, I've always given them the opportunity to change my mind from the certitude that they were frauds.

The first of these came when I was asked by the editor of a glossy magazine to profile a woman who, the editor had been told, was "the world's unlikeliest Hollywood insider"—an unassuming psychic who lived and worked in an inner-city neighborhood but who, nevertheless, counted a large number of celebrities and film moguls among her clientele. Her name was Rev. Ruby Weeks (though I'm not sure if she was actually ordained or just liked the sound of the title).

My bullshit detector started flashing and beeping right away. Not because show-business types aren't so pathetically insecure that they'll do almost anything to get an edge (they clearly are); but I was having a hard time picturing the power-suit crowd hopping in their Porsches and limos to make the pilgrimage to South-Central LA, an area better known in the late '80s for gangs and guns than pathways to spiritual enlightenment.

The beeping grew louder when I arrived at her digs: a nondescript storefront located between the Duke and Duchess Barber Shop and the boarded-up Them Bones Bar-B-Que. It became louder still when Rev. Weeks, a soft-spoken, full-figured black woman wearing a wool pantsuit and an enigmatic smile, showed me her small, sparsely decorated workspace featuring a faded painting of Jesus, a stack of 8-track gospel tapes, and a hand-lettered sign that read "Donations $25, No Checks Please."

And it was fully wailing when she sat me down for a reading and I saw that she employed none of the mysterioso trappings one might normally associate with soothsayers—no burning incense, no crystal ball, no pyramids or tarot cards. "I'm just a regular person, blessed with a gift," she explained. "I don't need no gimmicks."

A regular person? No gimmicks? Twenty-five-dollar donations? Hollywood types would never go for that. They prefer their spiritual enlightenment with a lot more theatrics, gaudy special effects, and a gold-plated price tag. Think J. Z. Knight, the former cable TV saleswoman who made millions, and attracted celebrity acolytes like Linda Evans, in the early '80s "channeling" Ramtha, the Enlightened One—a thirty-five-thousand-year-old Lemurian warrior who appeared to her as a seven-foot-tall apparition of golden glitter clad in a purple robe. Now, that's showbiz!

But even if I wasn't buying Rev. Weeks's Hollywood bona fides, I was still open to having her demonstrate her "gift." So we settled in to hear what "the spirits" were telling her about me. She closed her eyes, took a few deep breaths, then said she was getting a strong feeling about problems with one of my knees—which were both fine. She also felt good about my current romantic situation. When I told her that I hadn't had a serious girlfriend in years, she flipped it and predicted that would change "very soon"—indeed, that I would be married by the "end of the year" (spoiler alert: I wasn't). By the time she moved on to a series of other unverifiable "prophecies" for me, I was pretty sure I wasn't dealing with the second coming of Nostradamus. This presented a dilemma: I knew the editor wasn't looking to have me debunk Rev. Weeks; she wanted me to plant the magazine's flag on this "discovery." They'd already decided to make my profile the first in a new series, "Mystic of the Month." So I wrote a story that stopped short of anointing her as a visionary but, citing "a number of well-placed sources," *did* portray her as an unlikely Hollywood guru (hey, a freelancer's gotta eat!).

I could not have predicted the reaction to the piece (and, let's be honest, neither could Ruby): it went the pre-Internet version of viral, and, even five years after it was published, I was still getting regular calls from all over the world from people who hoped I could put them in touch with Rev. Weeks (I guess my number was easier to find in the phone book than hers).

Sometimes the callers would ask if she was really "blessed with the gift." I found it hard to burst their bubbles; they so wanted to believe. At those times, I'd always think of the classic line from *The Man Who Shot Liberty Valance*: "When the legend becomes fact, print the legend."

My next close encounter of the paranormal kind was actually once removed—on a cassette tape recorded by my pal Skip. Unlike me, Skip is a both-feet-in believer. Now, I'm not saying he's gullible, just that he's never come across a road to spiritual development that he didn't want to hitch a ride down.

He'd been given the name of a woman who reputedly had a "mind-blowing" ability to "channel" spirit guides—that is, allow a "spirit being" to temporarily inhabit her body for the purpose of delivering advice and other messages from those who'd taken up residency in the Great Beyond.

When he met with her, she allowed him to tape-record their session. It was so remarkable, I've kept the cassette in a safe place for the past twenty-seven years.

I feel absolutely comfortable in saying that it is one of the funniest recordings in history—just a few notches below the best of Pryor, Carlin, and the 2,000 Year Old Man but above Grammy-winning classics like *The Button-Down Mind of Bob Newhart* and Flip Wilson's *The Devil Made Me Buy This Dress.*

The thing that makes it so extraordinary is the channeler's unique ability to combine atrocious acting, a shocking lack of knowledge of things she's talking about, and the absence of even a scintilla of shame.

To fully appreciate the tape's genius, you need to hear the performance. But I'll do my best to describe what occurred.

After dispensing with some preliminaries, the woman asks Skip what he'd like guidance on. He says it would be nice to get some insights into his acting career. She says she'll go see who in the spirit world might be able to help. After a short silence, during which she appears to be going into some kind of trance, she begins speaking in a stentorian theatrical voice with a vaguely British accent.

"Hello," she says. "My name is John Barrymore, of the acting Barrymore family. Perhaps you are familiar with my work."

Skip replies: "Yes, I am." It's clear he's trying hard to be polite.

"Barrymore" then proceeds, in the hammiest delivery outside of a Nic Cage film festival, to offer the following show-business tips:

"A good resume is very important . . . So is a good head shot."

"A well-connected manager can help."

"Always go into an audition thinking you'll get the role."

"Knowing your lines will help you relax."

"A bad dress rehearsal means you'll have a great opening night."

I'll never know how Skip kept from laughing. After "Barrymore" is done, the channeler returns and asks Skip what else he'd like to know. Good manners are all that keep him from replying: "Can I get a refund?" Instead, he gamely tells her that he'd like to know anything he can about his father, who had died in a plane crash five years earlier. She asks what Skip's dad had done for a living and he tells her he'd been in "the oil business."

She goes back into trance mode, then starts speaking again, this time in a ludicrous voice that is a high-pitched cross between Walter Brennan and Gabby Hayes. Her performance is straight out of an adult education improv class; it's so amateurish it makes her "Barrymore" look like a towering work of nuance and subtlety. Here is a verbatim transcript of her opening riff:

"Hello, pardner . . . My name is Wee Willie Winky. Yessir, I'm an old time wildcattin' oil man. Worked the Oklahoma Territory back in the day. Also worked some in Texas and Loo-ee-zee-anna. Yessir, folks in them parts all knew Wee Willie Winky!!"

I've never been able to make it through all of "Wee Willie's" monologue without having to turn off the tape to catch my breath from laughing so hard. It has also put me as close as I've come to peeing in my pants since my uncle used to tickle me, asking "Are you ticklish or Jewish?" (I never understood why I had to choose.)

But "Wee Willie" did offer the following "wildcatter wisdom":

"Sometimes you hit a geyser; other times you come up dry. Important thing is to keep drillin'."

"Ain't no better feelin' than hitting a gusher; makes all them duds worth the effort."

"It's like ol' John D. Rockefeller always said, 'the way to get rich is get up early, work late—and strike oil!'"

Skip didn't have it in him to ask "Wee Willie" about his dad. After "Wee Willie" moseyed back to the Big Oil Field in the Sky with a chirpy "Happy trails, amigo!" the channeler returned and Skip quickly ended the session.

He came directly to my house to play me the tape. He was a little embarrassed that he'd paid the woman her one-hundred-dollar fee but, between belly laughs, I assured him it was worth every penny.

A couple of years later, I had hit a bit of a plateau in my personal and professional lives. So I was more susceptible than usual when another buddy of mine called to tell me that he'd just seen "an unreal" psychic who had "absolutely nailed it. She read me like a book. Deep shit too. Trust me, this was better than a year of therapy."

His fervor, coupled with my sense that I was stuck in a rut and could use a push, overcame my congenital dubiousness. I made an appointment for the next day.

I began to question my decision as soon as I pulled up in front of her home. It was a small, dilapidated house with peeling paint, shutters with missing shingles, and an overgrown front yard. A rusted old car sat on blocks in the driveway. I immediately thought of the Jay Leno line: "How come you never see a headline like 'Psychic Wins Lottery'?"

The woman, whose name was Doris, looked as shabby as her house. Her bleached-blonde hair was thinning, as was the fabric on her pink-and-white tracksuit. A cigarette dangled from her lips, while a tiny high-strung dog with matted fur yapped at her feet.

I will occasionally utter the phrase "I try not to be judgmental," but who the fuck am I kidding?—I'm more judgmental than a Baptist preacher at a dirty-dancing contest. I've delivered more verdicts than Judge Judy and Judge Wapner combined. And I'd already rendered my ruling on Doris: crackpot. But maybe she was a crackpot with supernatural powers, so we took a seat in her kitchen.

Doris had asked me to bring along objects belonging to people I wanted her to "read." The first item I handed her was a man's wristwatch. She held it in her palm, closed her eyes, then asked: "Is this your watch?" My first thought was, *You need a hint already?* I immediately flashed on the feeling I've occasionally had when I've booked a massage at a hotel spa and as soon as the therapist starts rubbing my back I can instantly tell it's going to be a shitty massage, and I think, *Oh, crap, now I gotta lie here for a whole hour and pretend I'm not miserable.*

"Yep," I said, "that's my watch."

She then proceeded to give me a perfect reading; and by "perfect" I mean that she was 100 percent wrong about everything she said. She couldn't have been more wrong if someone had told her they were going to kill her yapping dog if she came within a mile of saying even a syllable that rang true.

I'd also brought with me a copy of a screenplay I'd sold to a movie studio but that was stuck in Development Hell. Doris held the script and told me she was certain that "NBC is going to buy this in the near future." I explained that it was a feature film script, not a TV show, and that its story line and language would probably make it R-rated, so not really suitable for a broadcast network. But she was steadfast: *NBC is going to buy this script!* The banalities dispensed by "Wee Willie" and "Barrymore" popped into my head and I thought: If you are going to try to bullshit people for a living, Doris, shouldn't you and your fellow fraudsters have at least a rudimentary understanding of the things you spout off about? But maybe self-delusion was the true gift these bogus psychics possessed.

I was ready to call it a day when Doris noticed a third object I'd brought—a ring belonging to my girlfriend, Tammy. She held out her hand and I reluctantly gave it to her, ready for another round of malarkey.

As soon as Doris closed her fingers around the ring, her eyes lit up as if she'd been zapped by a small electrical charge. "Delightful," she exclaimed. "The person who this ring belongs to is absolutely delightful!"

Now, she could have used dozens of words that accurately described my girlfriend: warm, lovely, sweet, generous, kind, compassionate, smart, funny, considerate, pretty, charming, and thoughtful all would have fit. But of the multitude of adjectives in the English language, "delightful" was the one that most perfectly captured Tammy's essence.

I noticed that Doris was wearing the same expression on her face as Whoopi Goldberg's con artist medium had in *Ghost* when she realized she was actually communicating with Patrick Swayze's spirit. It screamed: *Is this really happening?* "Whatever you do," she told me with a vehemence that I think caught her by surprise, "don't let this girl get away. She's the one for you!"

At that point, Tammy and I been dating for two years and living together for one. We both knew that the next step was getting engaged, and each of us had, at different times, questioned whether we were ready to make that lifetime commitment.

Doris handed me back the ring and stared into my eyes. I became aware that the ratty little dog had stopped yapping and was also gazing up at me.

It was as if the mutt wanted to tell me: "Dude, she pulled the rest of this reading out of her ass, but she's actually feeling this one!"

Of course, I understand that Doris taking a woman's ring and declaring its owner—likely a lover, possibly a mother—"delightful" isn't exactly Jules Verne predicting the Apollo moon landing one hundred years before it happened (it's more like telling someone it looks like they've lost weight; who doesn't want to hear that?). And it's not the reason I proposed to Tammy a few months later—or have enjoyed twenty-five years of a delightful marriage to her.

But there was something about that moment that felt different from any I'd ever experienced. Something far beyond the old adage about even a stopped clairvoyant being right twice a day.

Over the ensuing two decades, I didn't interact with any more self-proclaimed psychics, other than avoiding the random rent-a-soothsayer at a birthday bash or bar mitzvah.

I continued to wear my skepticism as a badge of honor—with one guilty-pleasure exception. Every now and then, I got a kick out of watching *Long Island Medium*, the TV show in which thick-accented, blonde-bouffant-coiffed Theresa Caputo—who claims to possess psychic abilities—talks to assorted dead people, bringing messages of hope and healing to those they left behind.

It's hokey and manipulative, expertly engineered to tug at the heartstrings of even a die-hard cynic. And it's damn good television. I'll admit to shedding more than a random tear watching it.

That's not to imply I believed her "I talk to dead people" shtick, just that she was a virtuoso at it. My wife wasn't as sure, and was excited to learn that we had booked Theresa as a guest on HuffPost Live. She wanted me to see if Theresa could connect with my father, who had died two years earlier.

My dad had been a big part of our lives and, since his passing, my wife had sometimes felt his presence in more than just our memories—that he was now and then letting us know he was around by causing a pencil to roll off a table, or moving keys or eyeglasses that she was sure "hadn't been there before."

I thought this was sweet but nothing more than wishful thinking. But while Theresa was being interviewed on our set, I impulsively decided to stop by the green room to say hello before she left. On her show, Theresa often approaches random people—at restaurants, the dry cleaners, on the sidewalk—because her otherworldly guide, what she calls "Spirit," has a message for them. Maybe the same thing would happen with me.

My thinking was, *I don't believe in this shit . . . but why not see what she says?* If anyone could send a message from the other side, it would be my dad, who had an enormous personality even the afterlife would have a hard time containing.

When our producer, who was leading Theresa back to the green room, spotted me hovering in the doorway, she introduced us. I said hello, all the time picturing my dad floating in the air above us. Nothing. So I followed Theresa into the green room, making small talk while she gathered her things. I continued to think Dad thoughts. Still nothing. I kept this up as I escorted Theresa and her small entourage to the elevators. I thought to myself, *Okay, Dad, you always had something to say . . . so let her rip. It's now or never . . .* But Theresa, who was always so chatty on the show, and always seemed so happy to deliver otherworldly communiques, didn't say a thing other than "Bye." The elevator doors slid shut. Maybe she only hears from Spirit when the TLC cameras are rolling.

As I walked back to our studio, two emotions wrestled for control of my heart: satisfaction that my lifelong belief in disbelief had been validated, and disappointment that Theresa hadn't heard from my dad.

Disappointment won the bout; sometimes you don't want to be proved right.

As I stepped into my office, a pen rolled off the desk and hit the floor. I couldn't help but laugh—that would be just like my contrarian father; he wouldn't send a message through a TV medium. That would be too obvious. A putz move. Much cooler to telekinetically propel a ballpoint.

I picked up the pen and slid it behind my ear. Just in case.

The Big Queasy

Sitting in the corner of a French Quarter apartment at 3:00 a.m., grinding my teeth, trying to will my racing heart to slow down, and watching a roomful of strangers snort lines of cocaine I'd just sold them, I had only one thought: *Fuck you, Prince Charles!*

He didn't know it, of course, but his "fairy-tale wedding" to Lady Diana had landed me in the midst of the most bizarre three days of my life.

The wheels of weirdness had actually been set in motion six months earlier when I met a woman named Susan at a dance club in Fort Lauderdale where she was vacationing with a friend, and I was looking to pick up girls vacationing with a friend. We'd danced, then hung out talking while my buddy and her traveling companion, who either had less morals or more libido than we did, had sex in the back of my car.

She had sparkly eyes and a spunky attitude, and we likely would never have seen each other again, except for the fact that she lived in the Pacific time zone, and thus was a perfect person for me to call when I got home from the clubs at 2:00 a.m. but was too wired for bed. Which I often was, thanks to the recent introduction of cocaine into my social circle.

Back in the early '80s, coke was still seen as a benevolent drug, a fun drug, a party drug. Nose candy. Freud's favorite. And South Florida was awash with the stuff. It was spread around as liberally as suntan lotion. I knew people who used it to pay their dentist, tip their hairstylist, or wrap up as a Christmas bonus for their mailman. Everybody knew somebody who could get you some Peruvian Marching Powder cheap. It was Six Degrees of Tony Montana, only with five fewer degrees and a runny nose.

Coke and I did not make a cute couple. For most of my twenties, my default setting was "bouncing off walls," so adding a stimulant into the mix wasn't a smart move. Instead of making me perky and peppy, it got me so revved that I just wanted to sit in a corner and pray that I didn't have a heart attack. Good times.

Luckily, I've never been an addictive person, so my relationship with *yeyo* was almost exclusively social. I mean, what could be more communal than inviting a group of friends to join you in the bathroom to snort some lines off the lid of the toilet? Outside of all the chic paraphernalia—spoons, vials, razor necklaces, rolled up hundred-dollar bills—coke's greatest selling point was its power as a tool for seduction. "Wanna go back to my place and do some blow?" rarely failed to work. Unfortunately, it almost always led to long, meandering conversations—often about the desire to get more cocaine—rather than jacked-up sex.

So a cokehead I was not. But I did it enough that I regularly found myself on the phone late at night, chatting with Susan about everything and nothing (with the sporadic phone-sex session tossed in for fun). We talked about seeing each other again, but it never led to anything—until Charles and Di's televised nuptials struck a nerve in romantic hearts all across the globe, including Susan's. After weeping through the royal "I Do's," she'd invited me to meet her in New Orleans in ten days, after she attended a family function in Mississippi.

I'd never been to the Big Easy—and had nothing better to do—so I found a cheap flight and was soon on my way to rendezvous with a girl I'd spent a few hours with six months before. I was carrying limited expectations . . . and a couple of grams of cocaine tucked into my sock, just in case she wanted to party. (At that point, boarding a flight with drugs tucked into your sock was still seen, at least among my social circle, as standard vacation operating procedure as opposed to a fucking moronic move that could've landed me in prison until I was so old and shriveled not even a blind, undiscerning con would want to rape me.)

My trip started with a bang—actually more of a crunch—when the taxi I was taking from the airport rear-ended another cab. When the two drivers started pushing each other while threatening to insert their respective feet in each other's respective rectums, I tossed enough cash to cover the meter onto the front seat and walked the rest of the way to the hotel.

Since it was August in New Orleans—saltwater taffy in a steam room is less hot and sticky—by the time I reached the hotel, I was on the verge of heat stroke. And the scene I encountered when Susan let me in her room left me feeling even fainter: for starters, the room was actually hotter than it was outside; the thermostat was set at "cauterize." But more unsettling than the temperature was the presence of a third person, lying in one of the room's two beds, covered in blankets, shivering with what I soon learned was a spiking fever. This was Susan's sick friend and coworker Patty.

I was having a hard time processing the situation. Why was there another person in the room, let alone another person seemingly suffering from the Black Death? Was Susan not expecting this to be a romantic weekend—or was she thinking we'd only have sex when Patty lapsed into unconsciousness? Maybe she'd panicked at the last moment and brought her along as backup, not realizing Patty had been bitten by an infected fourteenth-century rodent.

Either way, this was not what I'd bargained for. I did the calculations in my head—tallying up the lack of privacy, the unlikelihood of sex, and the hothouse conditions in the room, then multiplying that total by my germophobia-to-the-third-power—and quickly determined I needed to get my own room, even though I couldn't afford it. My parents had given me a break-glass-only-in-case-of-emergency credit card; surely this would qualify.

Susan was a bit taken aback by the intensity of my commitment to getting the fuck out of her room, but helped me find a less expensive hotel down the block. Once I checked in, and turned the AC as low as it would go, we started to fool around. I'm not sure either of us was particularly in the mood, but after the six-month buildup, it almost seemed obligatory. Who says romance is dead?

After a notably perfunctory roll in the sheets, she turned to me and with all sincerity asked: "So, where do you see this going?"

I might have said "Huh?" It could have been "Wha—?" Or I possibly let slip the newly minted John McEnroe classic: "You cannot be serious!"

But whichever it was, she burst into tears.

Flustered, I made some crack about my sexual performance often making my partners sob, but that didn't help.

Gathering herself and her clothes, Susan said she was just tired, that she needed to go check on Patty, and that we should connect later that night or the next morning. Something told me I had inadvertently booked a first-class trip on the Awkward Express—and that I might be spending a lot less time exploring New Orleans, and the Kama Sutra, with Susan than I'd anticipated.

I began working the phones, scrambling to see if I could convince one of my buddies to fly up and join me—"The room is already paid for!" But there were no takers. It dawned on me that this could be a very long, potentially lonely, five days. I thought about just going home but chose to table that decision until morning. For now, I wanted to see what New Orleans was like at night.

I was not prepared for the explosion of energy and jubilation that hit me as soon as I stepped onto Bourbon Street. A flowing river of drinking, laughing, whooping, cavorting people filled the thoroughfare. Bursts of jazz music escaped from open bar doors. It was a full-on bacchanal. I had to remind myself this wasn't Mardi Gras; it was just a random Saturday night in August.

As I mixed in with the crowd, aimlessly wandering around the Quarter, something about the revelry began to strike me as forced and manufactured—as if all the high-fiving bros and shrieking women holding their commemorative Al Hirt hurricane glasses over their heads felt as obligated to act like they were having the time of their lives as Susan and I had felt to screw. It reminded me of the faux frivolity that reigns at a Disneyland parade. I pictured these Bourbon Street merrymakers as the New Orleans equivalent of those big-headed Disney characters who wander the Magic Kingdom waving like idiots and posing for photos—only here the Chip 'n Dale shtick included vomiting in alleyways.

These thoughts were interrupted by Rapunzel throwing down her hair—or at least her French Quarter counterpart: three girls in sorority T-shirts tossing beads from a hotel balcony. I looked up and saw a collection of big hair, toothy smiles, and cute figures.

One of the girls, a petite blonde holding a red plastic cup, leaned over and called down to me in a Southern-fried accent: "What y'all doing down there? You look so serious!"

"I'm trying to decide if this is the best place ever or proof of the coming apocalypse."

This seemed to amuse the trio. "Maybe it's both," said a tall, thin brunette, her accent equally honey dipped.

The third girl, another blonde, said they were having a party and that I should "come on up." They didn't have to ask twice.

As I approached the room number they'd given me, I found the door ajar and a party in full swing. The suite was packed with young, casually dressed guys and girls; it seemed like every one of them was holding a red plastic cup. I drew a few curious glances as I made my way toward the balcony, but I fit the demographic, if not the prevailing religious denomination.

My trio of Rapunzels seemed tickled to see me, and I was soon holding a sudsy red plastic cup of my own. The girls were named Allison, Candy, and Traci; they were all sorority sisters at Tulane, and couldn't have been friendlier. When Allison, the petite blonde, asked me what I was doing wandering Bourbon Street "all by my lonesome," I gave them a comedic rendition of my adventure—including Prince Charles, the coworker with the bubonic plague, and the unexpected tears (I left out the perfunctory sex). They laughed when they were supposed to, and Allison was particularly sympathetic to my plight. Things were going so well, I found myself wondering at what point I should unleash the "I have coke in my room" maneuver.

When Allison went to get another beer, and the other two were greeting a newly arrived friend, I glanced into the room and noticed a tall, rust-haired guy staring at me. When I caught his eye, he flashed a big smile, toasted me with his red plastic cup, and motioned me over. After a quick round of *Who me? Yes, you!* I ambled over.

Still beaming, he asked me my name.

"Roy?" he said when I told him. "Cool name . . . Don't meet many of them." Putting his hand on my shoulder, he leaned his head toward my ear. "Well, Roy . . . we'd like you to leave." The big grin never left his face. I wasn't sure I'd heard him right.

I might have said "Huh?" It could have been "Wha—?" I definitely didn't go full McEnroe. Whichever it was, he followed up with: "We want you to leave *right now.*"

For the first time, I noticed that we'd been joined by two other hulking college guys, one of them sporting thick, out-of-fashion muttonchop sideburns. They weren't smiling. My heart did a quick tumble into my scrotum, then trampolined back up.

"Oh, okay," I said. "Would it be alright if I said goodbye to Allison and the girls?"

Still smiling, the spokesman of the potential lynch mob said, "Only if you aren't a fan of keeping your balls." I unequivocally was, so I handed him my beer cup and made a beeline for the door.

Once I left the room, I bolted for the stairwell and raced out of the building. Worried I might be followed, I took a zigzag path back to my hotel, double-locked the door behind me, and didn't leave my room for the rest of the night.

I did not sleep well. At one point, I dreamed that I was the grand marshal in a Mardi Gras parade. The float I was riding on was manned by clones of Smiling Guy and his pal with the muttonchop sideburns, and instead of tossing plastic beads and doubloons to the crowd, they tossed them my testicles.

The next morning I called Susan, but the line just kept ringing. Maybe Patty had succumbed to the Black Death. Or maybe she'd had a miraculous recovery and they were out celebrating. Or maybe Susan figured it was me and didn't want to pick up.

I decided to check out a jazz club I'd heard opened early. It was pretty empty so I got a table right next to the small stage. The world-weary waitress informed me there was a two-drink minimum. Eleven in the morning seemed a little early to start drinking, so I asked, "How much for a ginger ale?"

"Six bucks."

"How much for a scotch?"

"Six bucks."

Scotch it was.

Despite the early hour, the band, whose average age looked to be somewhere between ninety and never-gonna-die-mother-fucker, was fantastic; they traded solos like commodities brokers trade soybeans and rice. The two scotches on an empty stomach had me feeling no pain, so when the band took a break I followed the musicians outside to say how much I dug them.

I found them gathered in the back alley. They graciously accepted my gushing accolades, and even tolerated my Music Appreciation 101–informed blathering about Coltrane, Bird, Bix, and Max's Kansas City. At a certain point, I realized they were getting high—probably when the trombone player passed me the joint. I decided this was the coolest moment of my life, and took a major toke.

Between the scotch and the pot, I was getting super stoned. But it was a happy high. I stuck around for another swinging set—the band dedicated one song to "our youngblood from Miami way"—then headed out on unsteady legs.

As if ordained by the We Know You're Blitzed, So We're Gonna Fuck With Your Head gods, upon leaving the club I happened upon a mule, that, I swear, started to talk to me: "Wanna check out the Quarter? Got room for one more. Best seat in the house!"

I did the classic rub-my-eyes-and-shake-my-head move, hoping to sober up enough to give the talking mule a thoughtful response. I try never to be rude to beasts of burden.

"What'cha say, young man?"

That's when I realized the mule was just chewing on the bit in its mouth. The one talking to me was a lithe, yellow-eyed, leather-skinned man wearing a white panama hat. He was seated on the front bench of a fringe-festooned carriage. Behind him was a collection of blond, very pale-skinned tourist types. Even in my pot-and-scotch haze, I was able to figure out that he was asking if I wanted to take a carriage tour of the French Quarter. How could I say no (even though I was deeply disappointed it hadn't been the mule that invited me)?

I quickly climbed onto the front seat beside him. The other passengers, who turned out to be German tourists, eyed me blankly, even after I tossed a chipper "How cool is this?" their way.

And so began one of the most entertaining hours of my life. Our driver, Thaddeus, was a fount of local knowledge, all served up with a distinctive drawl and repetitive delivery.

"Over here is Jean Lafitte's house," he would say. "Now Jean Lafitte was a pirate. But he was a *good* pirate. They say the house is the most haunted place in all N'Orleans. Don't know about dat . . . but dat's what they says. Jean Lafitte's house."

Or:

"Comin' up here . . . is the streetcar named Desire. You might know it from the play by a man they called Tennessee, though he wrote it while he was in Louisiana. It used to run from Canal to Desire Street. It's a streetcar . . . and they named it Desire."

I spent most of the tour giggling to myself, and not just because I was ripped. Thaddeus was pure gold. The Germans, on the other hand, didn't crack a smile the entire time. I'm almost certain they didn't understand a word Thaddeus said. As I climbed down from the carriage, I patted the mule and gave it one of the treats I'd purchased from Thaddeus. In between bites, I'm pretty sure I heard the animal mutter: "Fuckin' Krauts. None of them have a goddamn sense of humor."

Later that day, I finally got ahold of Susan. After some stilted small talk, we agreed to meet for dinner at a restaurant overlooking the Mississippi River. The jambalaya we ordered was heavy and the conversation was even heavier.

I apologized for my less-than-thoughtful response to her "where's this going?" query, and she apologized for asking. She explained that she was going through a rough patch back home and that she had projected a lot of unrealistic hopes onto me—or at least the guy on those late-night calls. On the phone, I was Prince Charming, ready to ride to her rescue. In real life, I was an unemployed twenty-two-year-old trying to figure out what came after college (turns out, it was panic attacks and a lot of therapy).

She told me she and Patty were going to head home the next morning. We hugged and promised to stay in touch, but I knew we'd never speak again.

I was now facing another three full days—and nights—on my own. I looked into changing my ticket, but the only affordable option was flying standby on a super-early flight two mornings later. So I tried to make the best of things.

The next morning, I went back to the jazz club only to find a different band playing and a completely different vibe. The one thing that was the same was the bored-to-tears attitude of the waitress. I ordered two six-dollar ginger ales but left during the first set, struck by the futility of trying to recapture a magic moment from the past (even if it was only twenty-four hours earlier).

After taking a long walk along the Mississippi, and spending some time checking out handmade voodoo dolls at a local shop, wondering if it was too late to put a hex on Smiling Guy and Muttonchop Man, I wandered into a waterfront restaurant for a bite. The guy at the door suggested I sit at the bar.

When I saw the bartender, I was glad he did. She was adorable, with a tumble of curly brown hair, a dimple on one side of her pouty mouth, and a raspy voice that sounded like it spent a lot of time shouting over loud music. Her name was Liz, and she had perfected an easy flirtiness that could be a gold mine for bartenders, waitresses, strippers, and other occupations fueled by gratuities and foolish men.

As she ping-ponged between a pair of guys at the other end of the bar and me, we chatted about what I was doing in New Orleans—the Prince Charles and bubonic plague stuff went over as well as it had with the girls on the balcony. When she found out I was from Miami, the conversation turned to drugs—and how much more plentiful coke was in Miami than New Orleans. Which was my cue to mention that I just might have some. In less time than it would take Thaddeus to say "Jean Lafitte's house," Liz had invited me to come to her place that night and "hang out" until my standby flight the next morning.

Back at my hotel, I giddily packed my bags while trying to determine how much of Liz's invitation was based on my charm and overall cuteness, and how much was based on the drugs. I'd be fine with 50/50—or even 60/40 coke. Any more than that and I'd feel bad about myself. I'd still go, of course, but I wouldn't be as cocky about it.

When I arrived at Liz's apartment, she'd just gotten out of the shower. She was wearing cutoff short shorts, a T-shirt, and a towel wrapped around her head. If my libido had a hand, it would've been high-fiving my ego. This night was going to redeem my whole misbegotten trip.

Liz poured us each a glass of wine and, after waiting long enough to build anticipation but not so long that I seemed like a coke-tease, I pulled out a small glass vial with a tiny gold spoon attached to the cap by an even tinier chain. Talk about adorable drug paraphernalia!

We each did a few spoonfuls of the white powder; she couldn't get over "how good this stuff" was. I talked about the drug scene in Miami, trying to come across like I was in the know without sounding like I was good buds with Pablo Escobar. As we took a few more snorts, I was also trying to calculate the precise moment when she might be open to me propositioning her but before the coke set us off on a conversational tangent we might never return from.

Before I formulated an answer, Liz turned to me and with a twinkle in her eye asked: "Would it be okay if I invited a friend to join us? He lives two floors up and this shit would blow his mind. In fact, if you had any more I'm sure he'd wanna buy it—at New Orleans prices" (which, she'd already told me, were four times what I'd paid).

This was clearly not the scenario I had in mind, especially since the way she said "friend" made me think there was something more between them. But what was I going to say—"Oh, I'd rather you didn't . . . I'm afraid his presence might have a negative impact on your desire to hump my brains out"?

A call was made and we were soon joined by Gino, a tall, swarthy guy with disconcertingly white teeth. He was very excited by the prospect of "some unstepped-on Miami flake." After doing a line off the glass coffee table and rubbing some on his gums—"Man, I love the freeze!" he said, smacking his fingertips with his numbed lips like a cartoon Italian chef in a frozen-pizza commercial—he indeed offered to buy more if I had it. So I sold him half a gram for twice what I'd paid for a full one. To his credit, he immediately laid out the coke he'd just bought and offered me the first hit.

I was already starting to feel wired, so I passed but thanked him for his generosity. He and Liz quickly hoovered up the small pile. Music was put on; more wine was drunk. My hopes for an erotic encounter had left my head and were now sitting on the couch next to Gino, openly mocking me.

When the coke was gone, Gino and Liz started trying to figure out if they knew anybody who might be able to get them more—even though "no way it would be as good as your shit, Roy." I told them I had another gram. You would've thought that I'd just announced I'd simultaneously discovered the cure for cancer and got the remaining Beatles to reunite.

Another call was placed and, before I knew it, three more friends of Liz and Gino had arrived. Everyone was having a blast. People kept thanking me and congratulating me on the quality of the coke—as if I'd personally grown and harvested it.

The drug had its usual effect on me: I went from upbeat and funny to overamped and neurotic. So I took a seat in the corner of the living room, doing my best to slow my heart rate while watching everyone else party.

As I unconsciously ground my back teeth, I did a quick mental accounting of my sixty hours in New Orleans: I'd been in a car wreck; had obligatory sex with a woman I barely knew, but had flown nine hundred miles to see, which ended with her in tears; gotten high with a group of ancient jazz musicians; chatted with a talking mule; stood beside the streetcar named Desire bellowing "Stella!"; come close to being tossed off the balcony of a Bourbon Street hotel by a bunch of drunk frat boys; and been invited to spend the night with—but, it turns out, not sleep with—a sexy bartender. Oh, and turned a decent profit by selling her friends drugs I was then invited to share.

Upon further review, maybe I owed Prince Charles and Lady Di an apology. Adventures like this don't come along every day. Or maybe just Diana—Charles was still a world-class twit.

My All-Time Super Bowl Record

It was an unexpectedly crisp and windy January day, with a high of fifty-eight degrees—downright frigid for us Miami natives. But even more peculiar than the unseasonable weather were the circumstances I found myself in: riding on a school bus, wearing denim overalls, a yellow T-shirt, and a plastic hard hat, on my way to attend Super Bowl X.

I was halfway through my junior year at Coral Gables Senior High, and our school's marching band had been invited to take part in the annual sporting spectacle's pregame show. I was not a member of the self-proclaimed "Band of Distinction," having exhibited no discernible musical talent. But I *was* a pretty good dancer, a skill honed through countless hours watching *Soul Train*. My specialties were popping and locking (go-to move: jumping in the air and landing in a jazz split), and a more-than-serviceable Robot—routines put on display at myriad parties and school dances.

It was at one of these functions that Miss Moser, the faculty advisor for the Gablettes dance squad, had spied my electric boogaloo and hatched the concept for the routine we were on our way to perform: while the band played a medley of "Steel Drivin' Man" (in honor of the defending champion Pittsburgh Steelers), "Rhinestone Cowboy" (for their opponents, the Dallas Cowboys), and "That's the Way (I Like It)" (just because it's an awesome song), my friend Jason and I, dressed like approximations of the Steelers' mascot, would engage in a dance battle/shoot-out at "the Super Bowl Corral" with a pair of dancers dressed like cowboys. There would be popping and locking, with the climax being all of us simultaneously gunning each other down and "dying" by leaping in the air and landing in a jazz split.

When pitched the opportunity, I readily agreed—partly because the performer in me liked the idea of being center stage in front of eighty thousand people, but mostly because I was ecstatic to get the chance to see the Big Game in person. For free! The word was that we would have field-level seats—in the end zone, but on the actual Super Bowl turf, mere yards away from the likes of Franco Harris, "Mean" Joe Greene, Roger Staubach, and Ed "Too Tall" Jones.

Sports have always taken up a disproportionate amount of my mental bandwidth, dwarfing the next two runners-up: sex and worries about my health.

My dad was a die-hard fan of the Red Sox, Celtics, Cubs, and Bears—even though he'd never lived in either Boston or Chicago. He was born and raised in New York; he just liked being a contrarian.

He absolutely loved to hate the local heroes. In the early '70s, when the Miami Dolphins were the best team in football and "Dol-Fan Mania" was sweeping the city, he'd root against them vociferously—even though we had season tickets to their games. My older brother and I, worried that this wouldn't end well, asked that our seats not be in the same section as his.

His oppositional fandom was really put to the test in the 1980s when the University of Miami football team became a national powerhouse. Every fiber of his being wanted to root against them, but a winning team meant a big spike in T-shirt sales at our family's college bookstore. In the name of profits, he had to choke down his virulent anti-homerism. It wasn't easy for him.

My brothers and I took my father's love of sports to a whole other level. We weren't just crazy about the three major sports— baseball, football, and basketball—we also obsessively followed tennis, golf, boxing, ice hockey, pro wrestling, auto racing, and all the weird pseudo sports covered every Saturday on *Wide World of Sports* (cliff diving from Acapulco was an annual must-watch). We even tuned in for televised bowling, for godsakes. Being American kids, we, of course, drew the line at soccer.

For most of our childhood, Miami didn't have a major league baseball, basketball, or hockey team. And the Dolphins didn't come along until my brother was eleven and I was seven. This allowed us to be free-agent sports fans and throw our support behind whichever teams and/or players earned our affection.

The calculus by which this devotion was earned was complicated, mysterious, and ineffable—an amorphous combination of factors that included uniform design, hairstyle, off-court reputation, known political leanings, and on-field flair. Having a bitchin' trading card helped immeasurably (we were *major* collectors; we'd buy them by the carton).

It all came down to the player or team's "coolness." It's why I loved Jim Brown, "Pistol Pete" Maravich, and Walt "Clyde"

Frazier. Why the rebellious Dick "Don't Call Me Richie" Allen was my favorite baseball player. And why I preferred Jack to Arnie, Borg to Connors, and Ali to anyone else on the planet.

In the end, thanks in no small part to the storytelling genius of NFL Films—with its slow-mo artistry, pulse-quickening music, and narration by John "the Voice of God" Facenda—football was probably our favorite sport to follow.

As such, the Super Bowl was always a big deal to us, even before it became a national obsession. It didn't hurt that the Orange Bowl, our home stadium, was the site of three of the first five Super Bowls—and now the tenth. Or, rather, the Xth.

Game day. In the Orange Bowl parking lot, we watched as adrenalized ticket holders poured into the stadium. Mr. Ledoux, the Gables band director, had us wait in the bus until just before it was time for our performance, lest the swoon-inducing delight of seeing teenage kids dressed in ragtag Steelers and Cowboys costumes be subverted.

Finally, it was showtime. Streaming out of a dark, dank tunnel, we rushed onto the sun-dappled field—and noticed that only about half the stadium was filled (it still being over an hour before kickoff). But half of 80,000 was nevertheless the biggest audience I'd ever danced in front of by about 39,900.

The rollicking rhythms of "Rhinestone Cowboy" soon filled the air. We popped, we locked, we jazz split—jumping extra high and landing extra hard—and, before we knew it, we were done, running off the field to a smattering of polite applause. That's the way, uh-huh, uh-huh, we half-heartedly like it!

Giddy, and still panting from the four-minute routine, we were shown to our seats—and discovered, to our profound dismay, that our "field-level seats" were, in fact, well below the actual playing field, in a kind of end-zone ravine.

It turns out that, because Miami averages sixty inches of rainfall a year, the field was slightly slanted to allow for easier drainage, with a massive drop-off beyond the back of the end zone. Our bleachers were located at the very bottom of that slope.

History books show that Super Bowl X was one of the most exciting of all time, featuring a fourth-quarter comeback, a last-second interception, and a series of spectacular, acrobatic catches by Steelers wideout Lynn Swann, who was named the game's MVP.

But we saw none of it. Not a single play. Our torment was exacerbated by the constant oohing and aahing of the massive crowd. We couldn't even see the crappy, bicentennial-themed halftime show, which, in those early years, didn't feature the likes of Beyoncé, Springsteen, Prince, or Michael Jackson—but rather those paragons of purity and milquetoast entertainment, Up with People.

Our only distraction was watching the Goodyear blimp make repeated passes perilously close to the Orange Bowl's upper deck—part of the filming of *Black Sunday*, a cinematic thriller starring Bruce Dern as a deranged pilot who plots to load the blimp with explosives and detonate it over the stadium during the Super Bowl—a heinous act many in the stands would've consented to if he promised to vaporize Up with People in the process.

Final score: Pittsburgh 21, Dallas 17, Plays Seen by Me 0.

It would be thirty-five years before I got another bite at the Super Bowl attendance apple.

My do-over deliverance arrived in the form of Tim Armstrong, CEO of AOL, which was in the process of acquiring the Huffington Post.

He thought it would be a kick to sign the final contracts at Super Bowl XLV (forty-five, for the Roman-numeral challenged), where he was hosting two-dozen injured veterans from the Wounded Warrior Project.

I happily accepted, knowing I was older, wiser, and wouldn't be forced to don overalls, a yellow T-shirt, and a plastic hard hat—even though the Steelers *were* back in the Big Game. And I felt pretty confident that, this time, I wouldn't be seated in a ditch behind the end zone.

Sure enough, when game day arrived and Tim's assistant handed us our tickets, we learned we'd be watching the game from one of Cowboy Stadium's state-of-the-art luxury suites. Or so I thought.

It seems the Sports Gods were not done fucking with me just yet.

First, on the way to the game, Arianna asked for my help editing the blog post she was writing to announce the AOL deal. Okay. Fine. So we'd miss the kickoff. Maybe a series or two. No big deal.

But as we sat in our car outside the stadium, hunched over my laptop, tweaking draft after draft, I could feel the game clock tick, tick, ticking away.

By the time I convinced her that Tim was probably wondering where we were, the second quarter was half over. Tick, tick, tick . . .

We finally made it to the luxury box and were immediately swept up in a flurry of activity—warm greetings led to multiple introductions, which led to multiple stacks of legal documents being presented, proofread, and signed.

I struggled to catch a glimpse of the on-field action, but the deal-closing was taking place at the rear of the spacious suite, far removed from where one sat to actually watch the game. Once again, I was at a Super Bowl and couldn't see a goddamn thing!

But I kept my powder dry, figuring once the contracts were signed we could settle in and catch the second half. That was when Tim suggested we fly back to New York as soon as the halftime show ended—once the deal was announced, there'd be a full slate of interviews and TV appearances, and we didn't want to get in too late, right?

Wait . . . *What?!?!*

I suddenly realized that I was in grave danger of repeating my Super Bowl shutout. I knew I couldn't possibly come to another one and not see a single play. So I rushed to the front of the suite, politely but insistently squeezing myself through the Wounded Warriors and their guests. In the process, I accidentally stepped on the foot of one of the injured vets. I was mortified when I glanced down and saw that it was attached to a high-tech prosthetic leg, but the guy gave me a cheery thumbs-up (also bionic). No arm, no foul, you might say—if you were a complete a-hole. Finally procuring a sliver of open space, I looked up just in time to spot Ben Roethlisberger drop back and unleash . . . a short, incomplete pass.

And that was it. Next thing I knew, the Black Eyed Peas were finishing their high-energy halftime performance, and we were on our way to the airport.

History, like Santayana warned, had repeated itself. It was like watching a boneheaded play instant-replayed on *SportsCenter* over and over and over again. This was the Mark Sanchez Butt Fumble of sports viewing.

I had now attended two Super Bowls—and seen a total of one play.

I'm pretty confident that's a record that won't easily be broken.

My Mother's Ashes

You know what they say: when it comes to disposing of your dead mother's cremated remains, the three most important things are location, location, location. And we were stuck on Important Thing One.

It's not that the discussion between me and my brothers had gotten contentious; but we were finding it more difficult to come to a consensus on how or where to spread her ashes than the UN's efforts to handle the Israeli-Palestinian conflict. And, yes, a Two-Urn Solution *was* discussed.

This was not our first human-remains rodeo; we'd scattered my father's ashes four years earlier. But that was an easier decision. Once we'd ruled out keeping him in an urn at the front of Book Horizons or spreading him around the weedy area outside the back of the store, we quickly agreed to disperse the ashes into the beautiful bay behind the house where he and my mom had lived for the past forty-one years.

We'd learned a number of valuable lessons from that experience:

1. A bag of cremated remains is bulkier, heavier, and denser than you might initially think.
2. My younger brother, Will, didn't want to have anything to do with parental ashes, or be a part of their spreading (though he did want to have a say in the disposition of same).
3. It's a lousy idea not to tell your teenage kids what you are planning to do with their grandfather until the last minute. The element of surprise will not work in your favor, even if the logic of "we didn't want you worrying about it this whole time" seems reasonable to you.
4. Wind is a crucial element to factor in.

But we'd sold the house after my father died, and the new owner had torn it down and was building his own—and trespassing didn't seem like a good charge to add to the already legally iffy proposition of dumping cremated remains off a dock into Biscayne Bay.

After a quick Google search, I found a boat we could charter that would take all of us—brothers, spouses, and children—outside the three-nautical-miles limit required by the Federal Clean Water Act. But the very things I saw as the upsides of this option, my older brother saw as drawbacks:

> Me: "We'll get to spend a few hours out on the ocean."
> Him: "But we'll have to spend a few hours out on the ocean!"

> Me: "We'll be in the sun and fresh air."
> Him: "But we'll be in the sun!"

Me: "The boat comes with a captain and first mate. They'll take care of all the logistics."
Him: "But we'll be with a captain and first mate. It won't feel private enough."

Countering, my older brother raised the idea of renting kayaks and all eleven of us paddling to the area behind the old house. But that seemed fraught with potential disaster (what if someone tipped over on the way and the bag of remains sunk to the bottom of the bay unopened?), to say nothing of a high likelihood of abundant mosquito bites, since the kayak launch was located in a mangrove forest. It was my turn to brandish the veto pen.

Fresh ideas were emailed back and forth. We knew we wanted to do something more than just find a meaningful place to scatter the ashes. We wanted to come together, to tell stories, to remember Leah Sekoff.

That process had begun for me three months earlier, when my younger brother had called to say that she'd died.

In many ways, it'd come as a relief. She'd been in decline for such a long time that I'd begun to think of her primarily as a medical patient about whom regular treatment decisions needed to be made.

As soon as I hung up the phone, I started to write her obituary—a project that soon had me once again thinking of her as the warm, funny, sometimes troubled, often wacky woman who'd raised us.

All people are, in their own way, complex (okay, you're right; let's be generous and say "most people"), a mixture of light and dark, giving and selfish, loving and cruel. But my mom took multifaceted to a whole other level. She was the human equivalent of a twenty-five-thousand-piece jigsaw puzzle, her personality a Gordian knot of quirks and contradictions.

She was vibrant, outgoing, and charming; but could also be withdrawn, depressed, and volatile. She loved to laugh—often until she couldn't catch her breath—but also cried more than her fair share.

It seemed like terrible things were always happening to her; but she'd invariably try to turn the negative into a positive, something that could contribute to the greater good. After a breast cancer scare, she founded a women's health-care group; when a flight attendant dropped a bottle of Cabernet on her head (leading to debilitating headaches), she got the airline to no longer serve wine on a handheld tray; after she got trapped in a hotel elevator, she lobbied for better emergency comm systems.

I always thought her biggest problem was being born a generation too soon, before women's achievements weren't dismissed with a societal "that's nice, dear." Her heart longed for the spotlight, or at least a greater chance to be recognized for her talents.

So she often told stories—almost certainly exaggerated—about glory days before she gave it up to become our mother: her time as a social worker ("I was known as the Mayor of the Bowery"); the time she "danced on the tables with the whores of Paris"; her work on the campaign of Henry Wallace. ("Not George Wallace . . . Henry Wallace. And we wore jeans before they were fashionable, when they were still called dungarees!")

She'd start a familiar story by saying "You don't know? I didn't tell you . . . ?"—even though we did and she had. And she'd usually end that story literally choking with laughter, unable to deliver the punch line.

One time, while out to dinner with a group of my friends, she was telling them about a new medication she was taking. It was effective, but it had one problematic side effect: "It gives me . . ."—she lowered her voice to a whisper—"dry . . ."—then raised it to a bellow—"VAGINA!!" When I suggested that, perhaps, "vagina" was the word to deliver sotto voce, she laughed until she had to grab her apparently parched nether region to keep from making it a whole lot damper.

She was neurotic, endlessly phobic, a world-class hypochondriac, and a one-of-a-kind character with an incredible zest for life.

And now she was gone, and deserving of a fitting send-off.

Since the whole cremation process made my brother Will, the only one of us who still lived in Miami, shudder, I arranged to have my mom's ashes shipped out to Los Angeles, where I'd hold on to them until a planned "Celebration of Leah's Life" a few months later.

When the package arrived, my wife was standing in front of our house, discussing our new drought-resistant yard with the landscaper. The mailman handed it to her and hurried off on his rounds. Tammy, caught up in hashing out the relative merits of organic wood-chip mulch versus decorative river rock, tucked the box under her arm and kept talking.

It wasn't until much later, when she saw the small "Contains Human Remains" sticker, that she realized, to her horror, she'd been nonchalantly toting around her mother-in-law's ashes for half an hour. To her credit, once she did, she didn't wonder, even for a moment, if the remains were drought resistant.

Now, maybe I have a very evolved take on death and have made peace with the ways in which our spirits live on, even after our bodies have been buried or vaporized. Or maybe I'm just an unfeeling bastard. But, either way, I never found myself imbuing the remains with any special meaning or value. They didn't freak me out; and they didn't fill me with sentiment. So I left them in the shipping box and tucked them on a shelf in my closet until the memorial.

When it was time to take the remains back to Miami, I double wrapped the sealed plastic bag they were in and tucked them into my carry-on. Knowing I'd likely be flagged by the TSA, I gave my kids a heads-up: "Grandma's in my backpack, but they'll probably want to run her through the scanner more than once."

And, of course, they did. First, they pulled me aside, loudly asking: "Whose bag is this?" Then they removed the powder-filled baggie that had drawn the X-ray agent's scrutiny.

"Uh, just so you know: those are my mother's ashes," I told the agent.

"I understand," he said. "But I still need to run it through the scanner on its own. I'll be as respectful as possible." I wasn't sure what that meant, but he gently deposited the baggie in one of those plastic TSA tubs, placed it on the conveyor belt, and sent it back through the X-ray monitor.

Even though they didn't spot any heroin packets or C-4 explosive hidden amid the ashes, they still did that chemical swab thing on my hands and backpack. Once that came up negative, the agent handed me back the packaged remains and said, "Sorry for your loss."

After much discussion, the brothers had finally landed on a plan: we and our families would take a driving tour of the three houses we had grown up in, then head to the cemetery where my mother's parents were buried and scatter a small amount of her ashes between their graves. I would then dispose of the rest of the ashes on my own (I was leaning toward a solo boat trip; "I'll get to spend a few hours on the ocean!").

It was a good day. Memories were jogged, funny stories were recounted, and the kids all seemed to enjoy seeing "the old neighborhoods" (or, at least, reinforced their reps as skillful social liars).

A highlight came when the owner of the house I'd lived in until I was twelve, a smiling Cuban lady, noticed the eleven of us loitering in front of her house and generously invited us to tour the backyard, startling and confusing her husband and daughter, who were playing in the swimming pool (somehow neither of them were blown away by our proclamation that we'd "put this pool in fifty years ago!"). Inevitably, long-simmering resentments over the time I threw my older brother's beloved stuffed monkey doll into the lake behind the house bubbled back up— the plea that I was "just a three-year-old" once again failing to sway the jury of one.

The only glitch came at the cemetery when, after locating our grandparents' plots (fodder for a run of bad *plotz* puns), and just before I sprinkled the small fraction of the remains I'd brought along, a graveyard maintenance man appeared out of nowhere and fired up his leaf blower.

Even though I assured everyone that I hadn't opened the baggie of ashes yet, more than a few of the kids were certain they had "accidentally inhaled Grandma Leah." In a way, the neurotic apples not falling far from the OCD tree was a fitting tribute to her memory.

That night a group of family and friends got together for dinner, drinks, and loving toasts. Old photos were passed around and, for a moment, I feared that they might include the one false step in my younger brother's otherwise stellar stewardship of my mother's well-being: the time he'd allowed her caretakers to enter her in the assisted living facility's Halloween costume contest, dressed as Dorothy from the *Wizard of Oz*, complete with a cutout Emerald City attached to the back of her wheelchair. The resulting photo—which looks like an outtake from a low-budget remake of *Weekend at Bernie's*, with my mother as the put-upon corpse—is something I'll never be able to unsee. An admission: when I found out that she'd taken second place, I *did* wonder who'd pocketed the fifty-dollar runner-up's prize.

By the time we got back to the hotel, it was nearing midnight. On an impulse, I decided that Tammy and I should close the circle and, taking advantage of the late hour and the lack of foot traffic on the jogging path outside the hotel, scatter the rest of my mother's ashes into the bay.

I texted my older brother and he agreed to join us. We were soon making our way along the seawall, looking out over the vast expanse of water, the lights of Miami Beach shimmering in the distance.

It was a warm and pleasant night. A half-moon half illuminated the sky. A balmy breeze gently rolled in from across the bay. We found a spot in front of a bench that allowed us to get fairly close to the water.

Jed and I each took hold of a corner of the plastic bag with the remaining remains. As we started to release the powdery contents, the wind suddenly kicked up. We hesitated, not wanting to reenact the scene in *The Big Lebowski* that ends with the Dude's face covered in his buddy Donny's ashes. *The Sekoff Brothers ⁄o not abide!*

I waited for the wind to calm down, then quickly leaned over the seawall and poured out the rest of my mother's ashes. The limited light made it hard to tell, but from where I was standing it looked like some of the remains didn't make it into the bay, landing instead on one of the rocks lining the water's edge. Jed and Tammy both leaned over to look, but they couldn't tell for sure either. A heebie tapped on my spine, but his pal jeebie didn't think it was worth getting out of bed for, and I calmed myself with the reminder that the tide would eventually come in.

The next morning, I returned to the water's edge and was mortified to see a clump of my mother's ashes still sitting on the rock.

Who am I kidding—"clump" is way too mild. It was more like a mound. In fact, it brought to mind the heaping pile of coke Tony Montana snorts near the end of *Scarface*. And, in this remake, I was suddenly the "bad guy comin' through!"

I sprinted back to the hotel and got a couple of bottles of water from the pool attendant, then sprinted back to Mt. Leah. I emptied the bottles over the cremains but barely made a dent in the stack. Indeed, it almost felt like it was having the opposite effect, as if adding water was turning the ashes into a ready-to-harden human concrete mix.

Starting to panic, I rushed upstairs to get Tammy—and more bottles of water. But when we returned to what we were beginning to refer to as "the scene of the crime," we saw that an elderly couple was sitting on the nearby bench. Avenging angels, perhaps?

We hovered, sending "oops, did I leave the stove on?" psychic vibes the couple's way. Finally, they moved on.

We emptied four more bottles of water on the ashes, with minimal erosion. This was starting to feel like some misguided science fair project gone terribly wrong: "The Unexpected Adhesive Properties of Human Remains When Mixed with Seawater, Algae, and Hotel-Branded Bottled Water."

Just when all seemed lost, the sound of a thumping bass line drew our attention. A sleek thirty-foot cabin cruiser, its sound system blasting Latino house music, was headed in our direction, slowly making its way out to sea. We were in a "No Wake Zone," but maybe, if it went just a little faster, or swerved a little closer, it could create a big enough ripple to drench the rock and wash the remains into the bay.

I shouted and gesticulated toward the party boat, doing my best to pantomime *Can you please pretend Somali pirates are after you?* Two sexy girls in string bikinis waved back, but the buff, shirtless guy at the helm left the throttle untouched.

Even though the boat was going super slow, as it passed, it sent a tiny whitecap our way. We began to cheer it on: "C'mon . . . Come to Momma—literally!" As it neared the seawall, the mini-swell looked like it had enough height and momentum to do the trick. But just as it was about to wash over the ashes, it collided with another, smaller stone jutting out of the water— redirecting the wake away from "mom's rock."

That little fucker! That's why no waves were getting to the remains: our rock was being cockblocked!

I started to formulate a new strategy—what were we on now, Plan G?—but then a thought popped into my head: maybe I'd been wrong to treat these remains as nothing more than residual bone fragments, the soulless residue of a vessel no longer needed. Maybe they did carry with them some of the spirit of the person from which they came—some essence of Leah.

And, if so, perhaps there was real meaning to be found in this moment.

What if this was my mother's way of holding on, of letting it be known that this was the spot where she wanted to stay? There was certainly lots of action—joggers, dogs, people on their lunch break. And, god knows, you couldn't beat the view. Maybe this was where her spirit wanted to spend eternity, forever telling her stories to the boats that slowly passed by: "You don't know? I didn't tell you . . . ? They used to call me the Mayor of the Bowery. Oh, sure, sure . . ."

Jewy Jewison and the Shabbat Shiksa

If I was looking for a phrase to summarize my Jewish identity as I was growing up, it would be "when convenient."

As the child of almost completely nonobservant parents, I was able to pick my spots: I was always more than happy to take Jewish holidays off from school, especially since we didn't have to spend them in temple. We'd just show up for the after-party at a relative's house and wolf down the chocolate babka.

Hanukkah worked; at least until my brother and I watched *A Charlie Brown Christmas* and decided we'd rather have our gifts delivered in a lump payment than doled out over eight nights.

I never failed to enjoy the moment during Passover when our uncle Dave would have to buy back the afikomen (the "stolen" matzo that was needed to complete the Seder). His daughter Margery always acted as our negotiator, and she was hard as nails. If his offer was too low—"What if I give each of you kids two silver dollars?"—Margery would sneer: "I'd rather *flush* the afikomen than hand it over for that little!"

And when I saw all the checks and savings bonds my brother got at his bar mitzvah, I instantly knew that the ages ten to thirteen would be my Yiddiest years on record.

But once the checks cleared and the bonds began to mature, I became more dismissive of my cultural heritage. I remember as a fifteen-year-old telling my parents that if asked to make a list of attributes to describe myself, "Jewish wouldn't be in the top twenty." To which my father replied: "Be sure to tell that to the Nazis when they are tossing you into the ovens."

Later, once I started working in show business, I was shameless in my willingness to toss out a Yiddish word or phrase in pitch meetings to subtly let the other person know that I was *mishbucha* (this was commonly known as Studio Yiddish. It also came in handy when a landlord was looking to rent to "a nice Jewish boy").

But, by and large, "Jewish" still wasn't in my top twenty.

Then I went to Grand Rapids, Michigan, to meet my lapsed-Catholic girlfriend's parents, and attend her ten-year high school reunion.

My Jewboy-hood started its climb up the charts the first time I met her mother (my future mother-in-law), a smart, kind-hearted, politically liberal teacher who tried to connect with me by telling me that she was reading *SeinLanguage*, Jerry Seinfeld's then-new book of humorous essays, and asking: "Wouldn't you say that most comedians are Jewish?" I wholeheartedly agreed, rattling off some of my favorite Jew comics: David Lettermanowitz, Richard Pryorstein, Bob Hopeberg, George Carlinbaum, Johnny Carsonheim, Bill Cosbyoffsky . . .

It took another leap upward at the Catholic Central High class of '81 reunion, held in the banquet room at the Grand Rapids AMF Fairlanes Bowling Alley. By and large, my girlfriend's classmates were pleasant, if a tad perplexed, regarding me as one might a rare bird that had veered off course during migration.

At one point, as I did my best to avoid the backup at the Salisbury steak station at the reunion's "family-style buffet," I found myself standing next to a tipsy guy wearing madras shorts, Sperry Top-Siders, and a *Magnum, P.I.* mustache. Three minutes into the encounter, upon learning that I was a writer named Sekoff, he belligerently insisted I confirm that "the Jews run Hollywood, right?" So I did, and reminded him not to forget the banks.

By the time I boarded my flight back to a place where a bagel wasn't considered an ethnic dish, "Jewish" was definitely #1 on my "describe yourself" list of attributes. With a bullet.

But it eventually slid down the charts again, where it comfortably remained through a nondenominational wedding that included stomping on a lightbulb (filling in for the traditional glassware) because it seemed like a fun thing to do, and the decision to raise our children as "secular humanists"—the offspring of a lapsed Catholic and a fallen Jew who found common ground in our respective cultures' veneration of guilt.

This all served as a precursor to the most profound shift in my Jewish identity, the result of buying a house in a predominantly Jewish neighborhood. Many observant Jewish families moved to the area so they could walk to one of the numerous nearby temples. We moved there for the quiet tree-lined streets, something of an anomaly in Los Angeles. It had a classic 1950s suburban vibe, the kind of place Ozzie and Harriet might live—except here it was Shlomo and Shoshana.

The farther you got from the temples, the less devout the people tended to be. Our block was slightly less conservative, but you could still have a picnic in the middle of the street between sundown Friday and sundown Saturday—aka the Sabbath, aka Shabbat—when most of our neighbors refrained from cooking, spending money, or operating appliances or machinery.

The pivotal moment in my transformation came six months after we moved in, when we drove down the block with a Christmas tree tied to the roof of our car; the looks we got made it seem as if it were the bloody corpse of Moses himself strapped to our minivan, or, perhaps, a team of Hezbollah terrorists disguised as a seven-foot Douglas fir.

It's not like our new neighbors had been particularly welcoming up to that point; watchful and wary was more the order of the day. But once we situated the tree in our bay window, the word spread fast and we were placed on what I came to think of as the No Hi List.

It didn't matter if my bright-eyed little daughter smiled, waved, and said hello, or if I tossed a chipper "Shabbat Shalom" their way, a high percentage of our neighbors refused to catch my eye or even acknowledge our presence.

Forget my bris, my bar mitzvah, or what the Nazis would say when they tossed me in the ovens, I was clearly not Jewish enough for these folks. In Grand Rapids, I was Jewy Jewison from Jewville; here, I was coauthor of *The Protocols of the Elders of Zion*.

The one exception to our customary ostracism was when an observant neighbor needed a non-Jew to perform a task they were prohibited from doing on the Sabbath.

The first time this happened, my wife and I were taking a walk on a sunny Saturday afternoon. Suddenly, the door to the house we were passing swung open and a woman stuck her head out and yelled to my wife: "Excuse me, you're not Jewish, right?" A little flustered, and not sure why she was asking, my wife hesitated before confirming she was not a Member of the Tribe.

"Good, then you can turn off my stove!"

This kind of thing began to happen more and more frequently, with my wife being called on to turn off lights, adjust a thermostat, and enter the code on a burglar alarm.

I started to wonder if this might be a good way for us to make some extra money. We could put little signs on telephone poles or slip flyers into mailboxes advertising her services. I even had a name and a slogan: "The Shabbat Shiksa: When God Says No, She Says 'Of Course!'" My wife doesn't believe in God but, being a much better person than me, didn't think it was a good idea to try to make a buck off of his laws—or, at least, laws that people thought he'd made.

But if he had made them, he certainly wasn't very clear about what they were. Indeed, if you asked twenty observant Jews what work the Torah says can and can't be done on the Sabbath, you'd get two hundred different answers. In truth, most rabbis say that no work should be done, even if you find a non-Jew to do it for you.

However, our neighbors didn't see it that way, and each of them drew the line in a different place. For instance, one of them asked my wife to replace a piece of tape placed over the sensor in his refrigerator to keep the light from turning on when the fridge door was opened. Apparently, in his mind, God had no problem with him using the appliance but would totally lose his Almighty shit if the little bulb went on.

Some felt confident that God didn't mind them explaining what they wanted my wife to do. Others believed he forbid explicit instructions. This led to one woman standing in our doorway smiling and nodding toward her house, but not saying a word. My wife followed the neighbor home but still couldn't get her to say what she needed. She tried guessing, a Talmudic version of charades, but the woman just kept shaking her head *no*. Finally, Tammy couldn't take it anymore and said, "I can't stand here forever. Maybe if you whisper it, God won't notice . . ." Turns out, she needed her to replace some candles that had burned down but couldn't be moved—except by the Shabbat Shiksa. "Of course!"

One Friday night as we were getting ready for bed, there was a loud knock on our door. It was a pious lady who lived a few houses down. Her husband, who'd been getting something in the kitchen without turning on the lights, had tripped and injured his ankle, and was going to need X-rays.

I figured she wanted one of us to drive them to the emergency room. But, apparently, God was okay with her getting behind the wheel; she just needed someone to stay at their house in case her kids woke up.

I agreed to do it and followed her to her living room, where I found her husband holding a bag of frozen peas on his badly swollen ankle. As she helped him hop to the car, a spiritual conundrum popped into my mind: Since I was a secular Jew, would it be okay if I watched TV while I hung out in their observant house? She said it would be fine as long as her kids didn't wake up and see it.

I told them I'd just read. But, after they left, I decided to go ahead and watch *Letterman*. I figured if the kids woke up, I'd turn it off, or point it so they couldn't see it (would hearing it be just as bad?), or maybe I'd be a rebel and give them a late-night Sabbath treat.

Or maybe I'd bargain with the little ones, see if they'd pay me to let them watch Dave, like buying back the afikomen at Passover: "I'd rather flush the Top Ten List than give it to you for two bucks!"

The lady and her husband were gone a long time. At a certain point, I went to the kitchen to get something to drink. I opened the refrigerator and saw a little strip of tape covering the sensor. I decided to remove it as a minor protest against the absurdity of the notion that God cared about whether the fridge light worked on Shabbat.

Then I spotted a small framed tapestry hanging on the kitchen wall. It was Anne Frank's most famous line: "In spite of everything, I still believe that people are really good at heart."

So I put the tape back. I knew I shouldn't feel good about myself for doing that, but I did.

Standing in the kitchen sipping a Snapple, I wondered what the neighbors who shunned us would think if they could see the mitzvah I was performing for this orthodox family—and whether it would make a shred of difference to the Nazis who were forever coming to toss me into the ovens.

Keeper of the Collection

After my father's memorial service, my brothers and I gathered at the family house to divvy up the task of going through his things and deciding what to keep, what to donate, and what to throw away.

My older brother picked photos, personal papers, and assorted collectibles (including the piece of shrapnel a medic pulled out of my dad's ass in Anzio).

My younger brother got clothes, business papers, and books.

I was put in charge of the porn.

I think it was less because they felt I had a special affinity for the obscene, and more a matter of their not being in the right state of mind to confront the psychological implications of what the trove of X-rated material my dad had accumulated through the years said about him—and, by extension, us.

Or maybe it was because I insisted.

Either way, later that night I found myself alone in the house, following in the footsteps of twelve-year-old me, in search of smut—only this time, I wasn't on the prowl for sexual titillation; I was looking to dispose of the evidence.

Not that my dad watching porn was a crime (if so, I'd be serving a life sentence in the Big Dirty House); but with a slate of real estate agents and potential buyers coming through in the near future, we figured an array of hard-core movies and magazines might not possess the interior design je ne sais quoi today's upscale home purchasers seem to prefer (*Oh, I love the granite countertops . . . and what they did with that blow job compilation is divine!*).

So I was going take on the role of "cleaner," like Harvey Keitel in *Pulp Fiction*; but instead of a headless murder victim, I was going to make a roomful of naked bodies disappear.

As I made my way into my father's inner sanctum, I half expected to be greeted by a guiding spirit: the Ghost of Masturbations Past. Out of instinct, I hesitated and cocked my ear, listening to see if I could hear car doors closing, the sign that someone was coming. Sadly, no one was.

Over the years, my father had gotten much less circumspect about his porn collection. While there were still a few items tucked away in the old familiar spot in the closet (including the ancient Bell & Howell projector, now covered in dust), most of it was displayed in plain sight on bookshelves in his den, interspersed with photos of family and close friends.

I imagine, for most people, there might be something a little disconcerting about seeing their children's smiling school pictures leaning against a VHS tape containing "The Best Sex Scenes of 2006." But I didn't think much of it—other than how cute my kids were when they had teeth missing.

I began gathering the salacious stuff and, soon enough, I was knee deep in a Whitman's Sampler of Filth. Dirty books, mags, videos, DVDs—there was even a well-worn 8-track tape containing a 1940s-style radio play, only with fucking.

Looking over the accumulated adult content, you could see the technological advances of the last half century played out in engorged penises and exposed vaginas: Super 8 film giving way to VHS tapes giving way to DVDs (my dad didn't have a home computer, so he apparently never made the pivot to Internet porn).

But whatever the format, the content was decidedly middle of the road. If pornography were a radio station, my dad would've been a classic rock DJ. His collection was heavy on the all-time hits: *Deep Throat, Behind the Green Door, The Devil in Miss Jones, Debbie Does Dallas.* It also showed a real appreciation for star power; there were lots of videos containing "The Best of" an assortment of familiar, above-the-title X-rated actresses from the Golden Age of Porn, along with a smattering of "next-gen" performers (my dad was never one to wallow in the past; up until the very end, he would call me to recommend a new movie, book, or TV show, always giving it his version of a five-star rating: "Roy, I'm telling you . . . *Don't miss it!*").

Interestingly, although his telephonic reviews covered a wide range of shared passions—everything from stand-up comedy to mystery novels to political satire to sports—outside of an occasional offhanded comment or jokey reference, we never talked about our mutual affinity for the prurient. It's not that the taboo was taboo; we just preferred to let sleeping Oedipal complexes lie.

When it came to porn, it's clear my father wasn't a completist—or a hoarder. Over the years, he'd regularly refreshed his collection. So what was now scattered across the floor of his den wasn't the sum total of his lifetime of licentious fandom, but rather the latest—and final—iteration. It wasn't a massive amount of smut; but it wasn't insignificant either. All told, it filled two and a half good-sized Hefty trash bags.

Once I'd gathered it all up, I was faced with the question: What do you do with two and a half trash bags of your father's favorite porn?

I didn't want to keep it. Today's instant online access to all manner of deviance makes keeping hard copies of hard-core content obsolete, reserved only for super-horny Luddites.

But I couldn't see myself just tossing the whole lewd kit and caboodle in the nearest dumpster either. For some reason, that felt disrespectful.

It reminded me of the time in my midtwenties when a friend told me that his girlfriend was refusing to move in with him unless he got rid of his porn stash, and he asked me to keep it for him "just in case things don't work out."

Who was I to say no?

Now, they say you can tell a lot about a man by the porn he chooses to own (they *do* say that, don't they?). If that's the case, I could tell without a doubt that my friend had really shitty taste in porn. It was almost unwatchable. Almost.

My friend and the girl eventually broke up, and I happily gave him his third-rate videos back. But the experience wasn't a total waste; it inspired me to write a spec *Seinfeld* script in which an acquaintance asks Jerry to take care of his "prized possession": an extensive collection of top-quality porn. We pick up the action soon after the guy drops off six large cardboard boxes of the stuff, and Jerry, George, and Kramer begin to pick through it:

GEORGE
Dirty magazines?! The guy gave you his collection of dirty magazines?

JERRY

This goes way beyond magazines. It's videos, books, audiotapes, postcards . . . the works.

Jerry flips through a three-ring binder.

JERRY

This is amazing. He has everything catalogued, indexed, and cross-referenced by title, date, performer, and perversion.

KRAMER

Look at that—he gives both the slang and the scientific name.

GEORGE

Jesus, I've never even heard of some of these.

KRAMER

The guy's some kind of sexual genius. A *sexpert.*

GEORGE

Strikes me as a little sick.

KRAMER

Oh, yeah—a sick, genius sexpert.

JERRY

Can you imagine the amount of time he must have put into this?

KRAMER
(*shrugs*)
Everybody needs a hobby.

GEORGE
So, you going to hang on to all this stuff?

JERRY
I gotta. I'm the "Keeper of the Collection."

Kramer pulls out a videotape.

KRAMER
So let's fire up the VCR and sample the merchandise.

JERRY
I don't think so, Kramer. Watching porno isn't really a group activity.

GEORGE
I agree. With people around, it seems silly. Alone, it's a blessing.

JERRY
It's like taking a shower. At home you luxuriate, soaping up all those hard to clean places. But at the gym, no way. It's the quick Rinse and Out.

GEORGE
You just can't be yourself.

KRAMER

I can't believe you guys! What's the matter—you afraid we might get so turned on we'll just start going at it?

Kramer chuckles. Jerry and George react: Bingo!

And . . . scene!

I had no idea if there was an aftermarket for this kind of collection—I'd never seen an estate sale for porn (although I can't think of a more appropriate use of the term "liquidation").

So I looked in the drawer where my dad always kept his phone books and was delighted to see that he was still old-school enough to have stockpiled the last few years' worth of Yellow Pages. I opened the latest edition to "Adult Bookstores" and saw that the place on Dixie Highway I'd remembered driving past countless times was still in business and open late.

I figured things might get weird—or hilarious—so I recruited Marcus, a fun-loving high school buddy, to go with me. He liked the idea of being the "Co-Keeper of the Collection," even if only for the night. (Given that Marcus was the only person I knew under eighty who didn't have a computer or a smartphone, I'd offered him the full-time role, but he lived with his octogenarian mother, who still liked snooping through his things, so he regretfully passed.)

Our jocular mood was broken as soon as we pulled up in front of the place. It was a small, squat, windowless building—yellow with red trim, and badly in need of a fresh coat of paint. The desultory signage promised "Video Rental, Novelties, Arcade, And More." It was seedier than a small-town watermelon-eating contest. The shattered glass and empty bottles of rotgut lining the parking lot didn't boost its curb appeal.

Neither Marcus nor I made a move to open our car door. The wisdom of this idea was quickly giving way to second thoughts. Without us exchanging a word, I put the car in gear and drove to a nearby dive bar that looked only marginally less unsavory.

An hour later, fortified by two rounds of drinks, we ambled into the dimly lit store. If the Times Square porn superstore I'd visited as an eighteen-year-old had been the Shangri-la of Sex Shops, this place was the tenth Circle of Hell (I know there were only nine, but if Dante's editor had seen this shithole he'd have demanded a rewrite).

I approached the front desk, manned by a big Cuban dude with a very small head, whose face was the spitting image of Hervé Villechaize from *Fantasy Island*—so much so, I was a little surprised when he didn't start pointing and yelling: "Ze porn! Ze porn, boss!!" Instead, he kept his eyes glued to his smartphone.

"Can I help you?" he asked without looking up.

"Uh, yes . . . I was wondering . . . Um, I've got a whole collection of porn out in the car, and I was wondering if that might be something you'd be interested in . . ."

He gave us a thorough once-over; he seemed confused.

"*Interested?* You mean as a potential viewer?" he asked.

"No, as a businessman . . . Is that the kind of thing you'd consider buying?"

"Not really," he said, turning back to his phone.

For some reason, his easy dismissal rankled me. It felt like he was insulting my dad. "But it's a very nice collection of stuff," I insisted. "Books, mags, videos, DVDs . . . Some of it is pretty classic."

"I'm sure it's the greatest fucking and sucking ever put on film," he said with a mixture of condescension and malice. "But there's not actually a demand for that kind of thing unless it's specialized kink or vintage stuff from the forties or fifties."

He exhaled sharply, and with a look I'd often seen on the face of exasperated professors, launched into a let-me-tell-ya-how-the-world-works-kid riff:

"Y'see, the motherfucking Internet has absolutely destroyed the porn small businessman like myself. I used to pay my mortgage with just the quarters I'd get in the whack-off booths. Now, that hardly covers the cost of keeping them clean . . ."

I cast a dubious glance at the dilapidated booths along the back wall.

"Clean-*ish*," he sneered. "And it's social media too. These days, everyone is tripping over their own dicks sticking dirty pictures on Snapchat, Twitter, Pinterest, Tumblr, and all the rest of them . . . And don't even get me started on virtual reality. Once that takes off, people won't even have sex with each other anymore. It'll all be robot blow jobs and shit like that." He shook his head disdainfully. "Your best bet is trying to sell your porn on eBay or Craigslist. But even that is a hassle; have fun writing up the descriptions . . ."

As the son of a college bookstore owner who'd seen Amazon take a sizable bite out of his business in recent years, I felt bad for the guy, so I bought a packet of glow-in-the-dark French-tickler condoms to try to boost his morale—but it didn't work. Back in the car, I offered them to Marcus, but he passed, so now I had one more thing to dispose of.

As we drove around aimlessly, I resigned myself to the inevitable and began thinking of places where I could dump two and a half trash bags of porn.

The choice of the collection's final resting place didn't rise to the level of trying to decide where to scatter a dead relative's ashes, but it didn't feel like I should just toss it all in the nearest dumpster either.

Plus, little dollops of paranoia started to release themselves into my bloodstream. Is it even legal to dump porn in someone else's trash bin? Is that a form of distribution of obscene materials? And, if so, would the porn be traceable? And what about kids—how could I be sure the smut didn't fall into the hands of an underage dumpster diver?

This was turning out to be more complicated than I'd imagined. For a moment, I thought about heaving the whole collection into the bay behind my parents' house—an echo of the time, as a teenager, I'd deep-sixed a lesbian skin flick that had gotten mangled in my dad's projector during a surreptitious screening. But this was two and a half bags . . . It would be like the Exxon Valdez of porn pollution.

Still, I had to think of something. I was heading back to LA the next day, and couldn't just leave the stuff in my hotel room or in the trunk of my rental car (again, too traceable).

We turned to Google for guidance and came upon a surprisingly robust online discussion about "How to Dispose of a Porn Stash," including a long thread on the concept of having a "porn buddy"—a trusted friend you disclose the location and extent of your porn collection to, with the understanding that if you suddenly die or become incapacitated, they will rush to your house and remove all incriminating material before your wife, girlfriend, parents, or landlord can find it.

But the online commenters were just as vexed as we were about what to do with the porn once you gathered it. "Burn it," "Dump it in the woods," and "Put it in a library's book return bin" were all popular—if problematic—suggestions. Enough people said, "Take it to the city dump" for Marcus to feel comfortable with offering to do so the next day, so we made the transfer from my trunk to his.

At the last moment, a wave of something resembling sentiment hit me, and I decided to take a few pieces from the collection ("a few" ended up being eight DVDs). Nothing with any particular meaning, just a few "classics" like *Deep Throat* and *Insatiable*.

As I pulled up to the hotel valet, I realized I didn't have anything to hide them in—so I told the parking attendant I'd forgotten something and drove to an all-night food mart where I bought a Gatorade and a PowerBar, which I quickly downed, keeping the plastic bag for my X-rated discs. They barely fit, so when I returned to the hotel, I tried to hold the bag behind my back as I hurried inside.

As soon as I settled into my room, I began regretting my impulsive decision to hold on to any of the porn. What was I thinking? Was it some bizarre effort to keep a small part of my dad close at hand—and, if so, was a '70s film about a woman who discovers her clitoris is located in her throat really the best vehicle for making that filial connection?

And, again, the paranoia: Was I really going to put this stuff in my carry-on? What if I got one of those aggro TSA agents who'd spot the DVDs on the X-ray machine and make me empty my bag in front of everyone, just because he could?

So I placed the DVDs back into the food mart bag and headed out into the warm and breezy Miami night in search of a suitable trash bin. It was past 2:00 a.m., so my concerns about the hardcore content being traceable to me or falling into an impressionable minor's hands were trumped by sheer exhaustion.

I wandered along the sidewalk for a number of blocks, surprised that there wasn't a trash receptacle on every corner—*come on, Miami, get with it, I have porn to ditch!* I finally spotted one but there was a guy leaning over it, digging through the contents in search of recyclable bottles and cans.

I decide to wait him out, but he was doing a very thorough job. He gradually became aware of my presence and straightened up.

"Go ahead, man," he said, glancing at the bag I was holding. "Throw your shit away. Unless it's actually dog shit . . . then I'd appreciate you waiting."

I laughed and started to move on. But he stopped me short. "You got any plastic, glass, or aluminum in there?"

"Uh, no . . . ," I replied. And then for reasons I'm not entirely sure of—probably fatigue—I said, "Actually, it's pornography."

"Pornography?"

"Yeah."

"You some kind of pervert?"

"Not the way you mean it . . ."

"So what's wrong with it?"

"Nothing, it's fully operational porn."

"Then why you throwing it away?"

"Long story. It was my dad's, and he died, and I was going to keep it . . . but now I can't."

"You inherited your father's porn?"

"Something like that . . . Any chance you'd want it?" I held up the bag.

The guy gestured toward a shopping cart filled with his possessions. "You see something in there I can watch it on?"

"Right. Well, maybe you could sell it."

He reached for the bag. "Lemme see what you got . . ."

He took out the DVDs. "Aw, man, you got some of the legends. Linda Lovelace, Marilyn Chambers, Ginger Lynn. You know she dated Charlie Sheen for a while, right?"

"Sounds like you know your porn star genealogy."

He just shrugged.

"They're yours if you want 'em," I said.

"Alright," he said. "No sense in just throwing good porn away . . ."

"Exactly."

I had half a thought of calling up Marcus and having him bring the rest of the stuff over. I could make this guy the Keeper of the Collection. But I quickly realized that wasn't practical on any number of levels.

So I wished him well and started to head back to my room. Then I remembered something. Reaching into my pocket, I pulled out the packet of French ticklers I'd bought at the porn shop, and tossed them to him.

"They glow in the dark," I said as if that explained everything.

And, from the way he nodded, maybe it did.

ABOUT THE AUTHOR

© Kristin Burns

Roy Sekoff was the founding editor of the Huffington Post and co-creator of HuffPost Live. A former writer and on-air correspondent for Michael Moore's Emmy-winning *TV Nation*, Sekoff is a frequent guest on TV and radio talk shows and an in-demand public speaker. He lives in Los Angeles with his wife and two children.

Made in the USA
Columbia, SC
10 June 2018